PLENISH

FUEL YOUR AMBITION

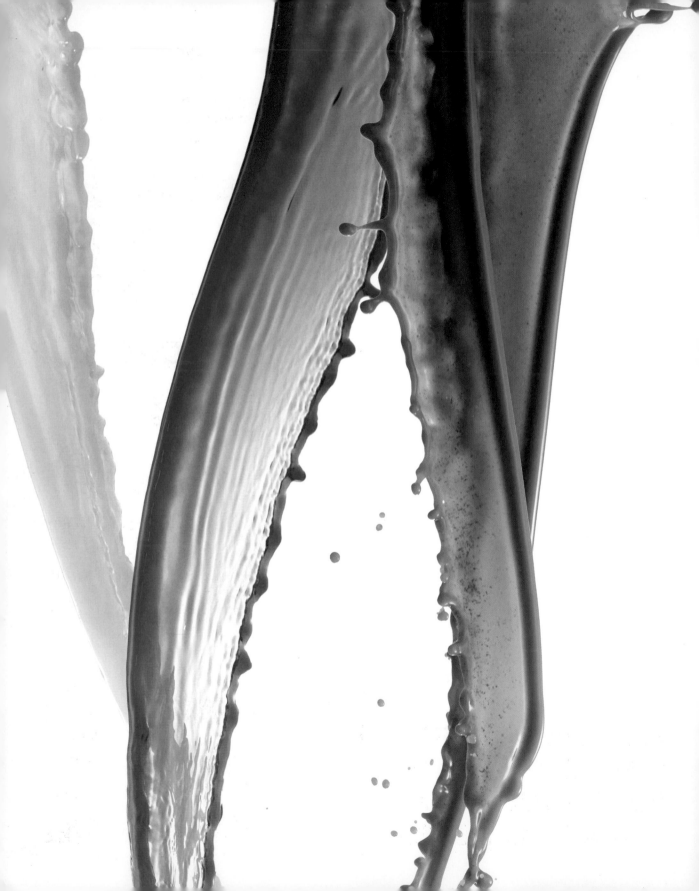

PLENISH

FUEL YOUR AMBITION

PLANT-BASED JUICES
& MEAL PLANS TO
POWER YOUR GOALS
KARA M. L. ROSEN

A Hachette UK Company
www.hachette.co.uk

First published in Great Britain in 2016 by Aster,
a division of Octopus Publishing Group Ltd., Carmelite House,
50 Victoria Embankment, London EC4Y 0DZ
www.octopusbooksusa.com

Distributed in the US by Hachette Book Group,
1290 Avenue of the Americas,
4th and 5th Floors, New York, NY 10020

Distributed in Canada by Canadian Manda Group,
664 Annette St., Toronto,
Ontario, Canada M6S 2C8

ISBN 978-1-78472-141-1

Printed and bound in China

10 9 8 7 6 5 4 3 2 1

Publishing Director **Stephanie Jackson**
Editor **Pollyanna Poulter**
Art Director **Yasia Williams**
Designer **Steve Leard**
Photography **Sam Hoffman and Chris Terry**
Food Stylist **Iain Graham**
Senior Production Manager **Peter Hunt**

CONTENTS

1. INTRODUCTION

8

Looking back, I can see that I was always proactive and had a strong work ethic. My last book, written when I was in my early 30s, was about the journey of eating well to cleanse and heal. Now in my late 30s, I can reflect that the last few years have been the most challenging, yet most satisfying, of my life. I left my career in magazine publishing, moved country, had a baby, and, several months later, started Plenish.

I moved to the UK to be with my husband a month after we married, leaving my home and job in New York behind me. During my 11-year career at Condé Nast, I worked around the clock and had the opportunity to express my creativity and hone my business skills. We did great work and were rewarded for it with upward motion. It was a busy but fulfilling career that I took a lot of pride in, and I suddenly felt a huge void without it. I hadn't realized how much being on a journey fulfilled me. Without it, I felt as though I was standing still, and I didn't enjoy the feeling.

I freelanced as a stopgap while I explored my career options and enrolled in some cooking classes to meet people and make delicious food (some of my favorite activities). I spent a lot of time looking for ingredients, talking to growers at the farmers' markets (hey, this is what you do when you arrive in a country with no family, no friends, and no job!), and learning a lot about the processes behind many of the products we buy off the supermarket shelves. I wasn't impressed. Being an avid juicer, I was also very frustrated that I couldn't find the organic, cold-pressed juice that I had grown to depend on in the US, so I started creating my own. My new friend Romi (another expat I had recently met in a post-natal yoga class), a talented dietician, was in a similar situation to me, and worked with me to create a range of juices that were not only delicious, but nutrient dense and low in natural sugar. We worked exclusively with growers who followed organic growing procedures (which reduce the exposure to pesticides and promote healthy soils).

A few weeks had gone by, and I was buzzing—partly because of all of the cold-pressed juices I was drinking, but mostly because I felt inspired by what we were creating. I started making juices for people I worked with, friends in my yoga class, and asking people for their feedback on how the juices made them feel. The feedback was wildly positive. Not only was I able to be creative, but I also found a way to make people feel good while following sustainable and ethical practices, and it awakened a passion and drive in me that I hadn't experienced before. I felt awake and like I needed to run.

Plenish was born from my own healing experiences via juice and plant-based food, and from my passion for sharing these nutrient-dense recipes so others can feel great, too. I was frustrated with the lack of integrity in most products on the supermarket shelves and I wanted to do something about it.

Since founding Plenish and finding a way to harness that passion and ambition, I've never been more clear on what we are PRO . . .

PRO revolutionizing the way we make and distribute food without preservatives and sugars. PRO supporting farmers who grow our organic produce without the use of harmful pesticides. PRO educating people about investing in wellness, not illness, and PRO building a brand that is a platform to inspire and influence real change.

As a brand we never stand still: we relish moving forward, because if you're not moving, you're not growing. Finally, we will continue to challenge ourselves to over-deliver on health and quality and make it more accessible.

Plenish has given me the opportunity to meet some amazing creators and entrepreneurs. A common theme among these ambitious people is that they have more passion and ideas than they do time. They rely heavily on diet and lifestyle choices so they can squeeze it all in. We will peek into the lives of some of these incredible people (see pages 42–59), who will inspire you (as they do me) to dream big and reach for the stars.

14

I am ambitious and I like ambitious people. Would you feel comfortable saying that out loud at work or in front of your friends?

Traditionally, ambition has had a negative connotation, particularly when applied to women. Ambition is often associated with being ruthless or narcissistic instead of being celebrated as having an insatiable drive to achieve.

Ambition is also commonly associated with financial reward, which for most successful people just isn't the whole story. When I was working an 18-hour shift in a juicing kitchen, it wasn't the idea of financial reward that kept me going; it was knowing there was a consumer who was going to have a positive experience with a juice or a cleanse that pushed me forward. When our first Harvey Nichols order came in, my kitchen manager called in sick. I worked through the night to fulfill it. The buyer gave me a once-in-a-lifetime shot and there was no way I wasn't going to deliver a perfect product. Do I want to have a profitable business and employ talented people? Sure. Is that the only driver? No way.

Channeling ambition into success demands extraordinary self-belief, determination (bordering on the obsessive), and often the courage to risk family and home when it comes to decision-making. Mostly, it requires a ton of hard work. So how do you fuel that ambition and turn it into a successful driver?

AMBITION IS NOT A DIRTY WORD

BE
AMBITIOUS

One of my favorite poems by
Edna St. Vincent Millay sums
up my perspective:

My candle burns at both ends;

It will not last the night;

But ah, my foes, and oh, my friends—

It gives a lovely light!

The more successful entrepreneurs I meet, the more I see that the common denominator is they all hustle, and I mean that in the most flattering way possible. They often relish chasing all their dreams—career, social, family—somehow getting it all done, even when it seems unachievable. They want more, work hard—and as they burn the candle at both ends, loving the light they've created, they need to make sure they don't burn out.

Ambitious people know that to squeeze everything in, they need to have energy that matches their drive; they need to feel well, eat the right food and nutrients at the right time, get regular exercise, and have a good support network. That doesn't make them machines.

They don't pretend to be perfect. They share their latest goals and their latest failures. They also know that a cocktail with the right people is as important as an hour in the gym. But whatever is in the glass, be it red wine or green juice, people who hustle see it as half full. And they keep moving. They may collapse into bed at night, but they're living at 110%—and who doesn't want that?

In the weeks when you know you're going to need extra energy, lateral thinking, glowing skin, optimism, and luck to get through, the food you put into your body is the secret weapon. And, if you veer off the healthy path (hey, we all need a little detour from being virtuous!), a juice cleanse or healthy eating plan will help you hit the reset button.

The most common question I'm asked in interviews is "How do you achieve a work/life balance?" (As a side note, I find this annoying, as I never hear it asked of a man.) The concept of balance has been the most stressful part of starting my business. I feel privileged to be the mother of a gorgeous and sassy four-year-old daughter, the wife of an equally ambitious and busy—and supportive—man, and the sustaining force behind the Plenish brand. Since Plenish started to take off, I have always struggled with how to find this illustrious point of "balance."

The reality is, it's absolutely unattainable to have all systems on full tilt at the same time. Sometimes you need to prioritize the most immediate or important task on hand. Some days I feel like a fantastic mom and wife. On these days, I'm usually not as committed to my business. Do I feel guilty? Sure. On the flip side, there are times when the business needs my total and utter commitment, which may mean that I miss a few drop-offs or pick-ups at school or am late for dinner. Do I feel even guiltier? Of course. It started to feel like a lose-lose situation where I wasn't doing a great job in either the work or the family role. The real loser here was me. I started giving up my early morning workouts to fit in an extra hour with my daughter, or simply to get into the office early. It just wasn't sustainable. I realized that following my passion and celebrating my ambition (versus feeling guilty for wanting more) allows me to be more fully present for my family when I am with them. On the flip side, taking time to give and receive love from my family and support network makes me feel like I can accomplish the world.

I wasn't the one who needed to change, it was this definition:

BALANCE
An even distribution of weight enabling someone or something to remain upright and steady.

There are periods when I support my family with all of my might, keeping them steady. In busier work times, they are pushing the scales the other way. I think ambitious people, particularly entrepreneurs, need their own definition of balance:

MODERN BALANCE
An *ever-changing* distribution of weight enabling someone to remain upright and steady.

Once I gave up the idea that I had to be equally good at all the pieces of my pie all of the time, I felt an enormous weight lift off my shoulders—and got back to enjoying (and being better at) all my roles.

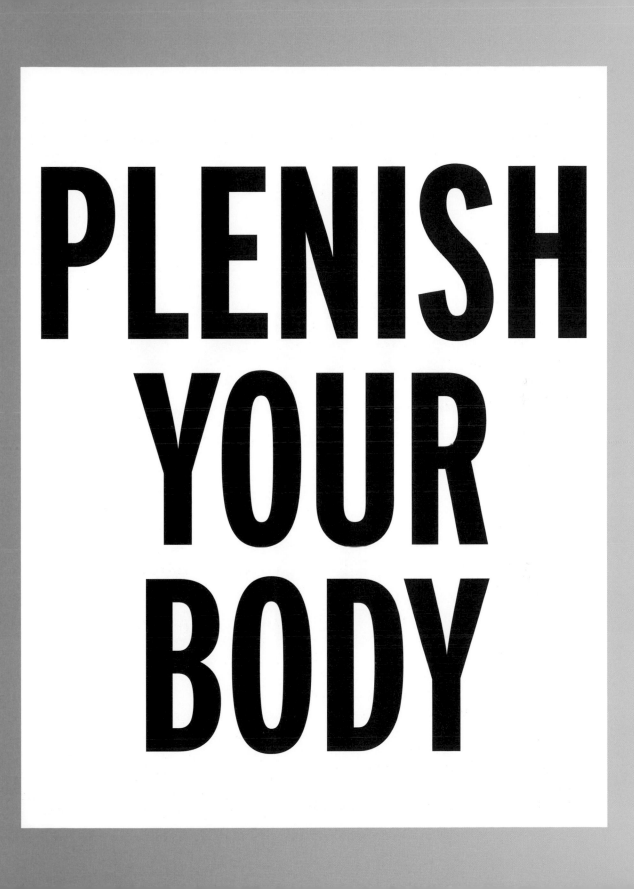

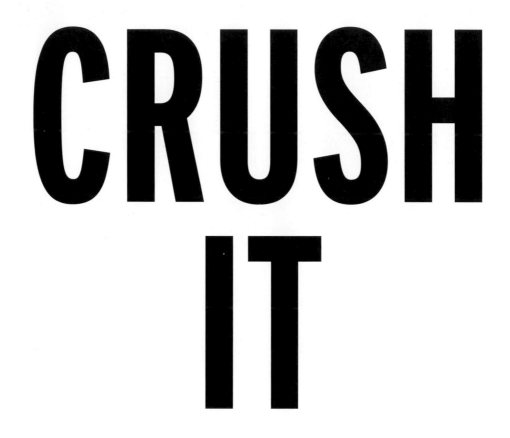

21

Growing the Plenish brand from a small, niche e-commerce business to one of the leading healthy drink brands in the UK has been an absolute labor of love. With more demands on me than ever before, I have to be mindful about supporting my well-being and mental health. I've learned to become aware of which foods enhance my performance and mood and fuel my ambition. I'm grateful to the amazing experts I've met over the years who have advised me on how to maintain my health and energy during these busy and challenging times, two of whom I've asked to collaborate on this book with me and share what we've learned with you. I hope the stories of some of our incredible Raw Ambition features will inspire you to dream big, and that the recipes and plans in this book can then enable you to feel fantastic enough for you to . . .

PRESS ON + CRUSH IT.

Kara

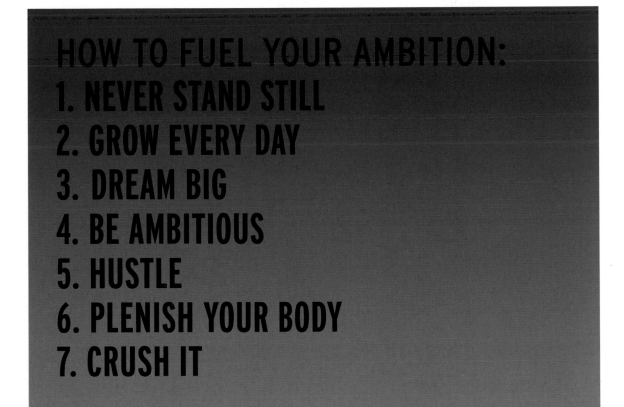

HOW TO FUEL YOUR AMBITION:
1. NEVER STAND STILL
2. GROW EVERY DAY
3. DREAM BIG
4. BE AMBITIOUS
5. HUSTLE
6. PLENISH YOUR BODY
7. CRUSH IT

2. GUT + BRAIN SCIENCE

EVE KALINIK
Nutritional Therapist and
Gut Health Specialist

Eve is a registered member of the British Association for Applied Nutrition and Nutritional Therapy (BANT) and the Complementary and Natural Healthcare Council (CNHC).

"My philosophy is working toward an authentic lifelong positive attitude of eating well. No quick fixes, fads, rules, detoxes, or diets, but rather a balanced and functional approach that supports the body on a deeper level to increase vitality and a consistent feeling of well-being for long-term change. And not to forget to enjoy the process of eating. Eating for the soul and connecting joyfully with our food can be just as important as what is on the plate in front of us.

I consider eating well to be one of THE most empowering things we can do for our health and self-awareness, and education is such an important part of this. As such I regularly host workshops, talks, and retreats with various media, corporate, and well-being companies. I also write regularly for leading publications and online platforms, tackling various nutrition-related topics that I believe are current, relevant, and can often be very confusing."

THE SCIENCE

The human brain is a complex and curious organ. An incomprehensible 100 billion neurons go into day-to-day decision-making, focus, emotional well-being, and creative flair. And while once upon a time it was thought that these brain cells cannot change or regrow, we now know that there is a constant repair and rewiring process throughout our lifetime that largely depends on how we support and care for our gray matter.

I've been working with nutritional therapist and gut health specialist Eve Kalinik for years. Eve started her career in PR, and is passionate about how food can really change the way you think, feel, and look from the inside out. In this chapter, you'll find the tools to make informed choices for gut health and mental performance, and in chapters 4 and 5 we've created recipes that utilize all of these foods in your juices and meals.

FEED YOUR BRAIN

Feeding our brains with the right nutrition has a much more far-reaching impact than you might imagine.

➕ EAT SMART

Everything from neurotransmitter brain chemical messaging to the health of neurons crucially depends on core nutrients functioning and performing at their best. Even that sense of butterflies in the stomach when we feel nervous or anxious about a deadline or a presentation is due to the enteric nervous system located in the gut. Some refer to this as the "second brain," because while it communicates to the brain it has the ability to independently change thoughts and behavior, too. The link between the mind and the gut is certainly a powerful one.

➕ WHY WE NEED CARBS

One of the main macronutrient groups the brain needs is carbohydrates, since it primarily uses glucose to function (hence that craving to grab a sugary treat when you are feeling mentally fatigued). In fact the brain uses around 20% of the body's metabolic supply but it is fussy about the carbs it likes, preferring the more nutrient-dense lower-sugar types, rather than the quick-fix treats. THE best carb choice is really vegetables in abundance. Moderate amounts of beans and legumes (lentils, chickpeas, lima beans), and some of the pseudo-grains such as quinoa or buckwheat, can be included too, but just make sure you put vegetables centerstage on your plate at as many meals as possible. Fruit is also brain-friendly, but again in considered amounts, so stick to one to two portions per day. Berries in all forms are great because they also contain brain-friendly antioxidants.

⊕ BUILDING BLOCKS FOR A HEALTHY BRAIN

Protein, or more specifically amino acids that form proteins, are essential to assist as precursors for brain chemicals known as neurotransmitters.

Think of these neurotransmitters as messengers that carry signals from one brain cell to another. Some of these will have a stimulating effect, others a sedative one. Having a diet rich in good-quality protein from as many food groups as possible (see chart below) should provide you with the necessary amino acids for these neurotransmitters to function optimally. Furthermore, inadequate intake of protein throughout the day can not only affect mental focus but will leave energy levels flagging too, so opt for wholesome natural sources at each meal.

FOOD SOURCES	AMINO ACID SOURCE	NEUROTRANSMITTER	FUNCTION
Pumpkin seeds, sunflower seeds, almonds, lean meats, eggs, white beans	Phenylalanine	Dopamine	Pleasure, emotions, mood, motor function
Salmon, mackerel, peanuts, sesame seeds, butter, lentils	Tyrosine & Phenylalanine	Adrenaline	Stress
Chia seeds, cashews, chicken, turkey, cod, eggs, spirulina, spinach, bananas	Tryptophan & Tyrosine	Serotonin	Sleep, mood, brain activity
Parsley, spinach, cabbage, fish, beans & legumes, lean meats	Glutamine & glutamate	GABA	Sleep, anxiety
Eggs, peanuts, spinach, beets, collard greens, chicken, shrimp	Choline	Acetylcholine	Memory, learning, cognitive function

27 ⊕ HEALTHY OILS FOR HEALTHY MINDS

The brain is around 60% fat, and it is these healthy oils that make up the components of cell membranes and the myelin sheath that surrounds the neurons. Getting the right amount and type of fats is a major part of brain health and performance. Fat is vital for brain health, and when you think that one of the richest sources of saturated fat in nature is human breast milk it makes a very interesting link.

You may also have heard the saying that eating fish makes us brainier, which is in fact true! This is because the cold-water types, such as wild salmon, mackerel, sardines, and trout, provide readily available direct sources of omega 3 essential fatty acids (EFAs), which are crucial for brain health. And it's the "essential" part of this that is important, since we have to get these through food. The most brain-beneficial of these comes from DHA (docosahexenoic acid). DHA is a primary component of the brain, particularly the cerebral cortex, which is responsible for processes such as memory, decision-making, emotions, and focus. In fact, studies show that deficiencies of DHA can be linked to neurodegenerative and mood disorder conditions, such as Alzheimer's and depression.

The DHA found in oily fish is particularly high, but it is ideal to get it from as wide a variety of foods as possible. Other good sources include grass-fed meats and poultry, free-range eggs, and algae such as spirulina. Make sure you get salmon that is wild, and that your meat, poultry, and eggs are organic, grass-fed, and free-range for the brain-health benefits. We can also find some DHA via the conversion of ALA (alpha-linolenic acid), the omega 3 found in plant foods such as chia, flaxseeds, and walnuts, but this amounts to very little in most cases, so it's always good to find a direct source to add in alongside this.

And while saturated fats have had a bad rap in the past, we need rich sources from natural whole foods such as coconut oil, coconut milk, and yogurt, ghee, organic butter, eggs, nuts, and seeds (plus their respective butters). Monounsaturated fats from avocados and cold-pressed oils, such as olive oil that has been unheated, are also excellent brain boosters.

✚ THINKING GREENS

Want to think better? Load up with vegetables! Brimming with the vitamins and minerals that neurotransmitters need as co-factors, vegetables across the board act as key team players. Vitamins such as B_6, B_3, B_1, C, and folic acid and minerals including zinc, magnesium, calcium, and iron are critical components of neurotransmitter functioning and they are found in abundance in plant foods.

Eating more vegetables also has a protective effect on our brains, since they boast a wealth of antioxidants that help reduce aging and damage to cells. Greens almost certainly check most of these boxes, so if you want to be smarter, get more greens on your plate. Berries and purple fruits and vegetables are also great for the brain because of their anthocyanin content, so adding more of these into your diet can help boost cognitive processes. And beta-carotene-rich orange-colored vegetables, such as sweet potatoes and carrots, also provide significant antioxidants.

Really, it is very simple. Eating as many different colors as possible is your best bet to get a broad range of these phytonutrient powerhouses. So, while "eating the rainbow" may be a cliché, it's still a pretty good mantra to follow.

IF YOU STRUGGLE WITH EATING A LOT OF VEGETABLES, ORGANIC, RAW JUICES CAN BE A CONVENIENT MEDIUM TO SQUEEZE JUST OVER 2 POUNDS OF THEM INTO YOUR DAY.

29 ➕ BEYOND FOOD

Are you getting enough light? Sunlight exposure and the resulting vitamin D production can have a lot of impact on mood and energy. Getting away from your desk even for a brisk 10 to 15 minute walk is a good way to top this off through the spring and summer months.

And the modern phenomenon of stress has its own physical as well as emotional impact on our brains. Cortisol, one of the major stress hormones, can deplete neurotransmitter messaging, so engaging in regular activities that put your body into a state of relaxation is an important part of performing well. It sounds counterintuitive to being more productive, but even small daily adjustments such as regular desk breaks and pre-bedtime daily breathing exercises can keep stress levels at bay.

BRAIN-HEALTHY FOODS

Matcha–contains EGCG, a powerful antioxidant that helps prevent damage to brain cells.

Spinach–a great source of magnesium that helps support the nervous system for a calmer mood while also maintaining consistent energy levels.

Kale–rich in antioxidants that help protect the brain from free radicals, as well as being an excellent source of B vitamins, which help reduce cognitive decline. And since B vitamins are rapidly depleted when we are stressed, keeping these topped off with greens of ALL varieties is important.

Nuts–all contain vitamin E, a potent antioxidant that helps prevent cognitive damage. Walnuts in particular also provide omega 3, which is linked to improved brain functioning. And almonds are a good source of tryptophan, a precursor to serotonin, a well known happy brain chemical.

Beets–contain betaine, which stimulates the production of S-Adenosyl methionine or SAM-e, which is essential in the production of dopamine, one of our feel-good neurotransmitters. The nitric oxide also found in beets supports better blood flow, maintaining sharper concentration and focus.

Cacao—contains mood-boosting substances such as theobromine, anandamide, and phenylethylamine, which all enhance positive brain chemicals.

Oily fish—the highest source of omega 3 oils, which help nourish and improve flexibility of cell membranes for enhanced brain neurotransmitter activity. This supports better cognitive processes, such as memory and concentration, and helps prevent neurodegenerative conditions.

Bananas—a plant-based source of tryptophan that acts as a precursor to serotonin, and they also contain B_6, which helps with this conversion. Plus they are also a good source of magnesium, and this helps to manage stress, too.

Broccoli—a cruciferous powerhouse that not only provides a wealth of B vitamins that help support better cognitive processes, but also contains vitamin K, which has also been linked to improved brain power.

Chia and flaxseeds—both contain ALA (alpha linolenic acid), a type of healthy oil that supports brain cell (neuron) health and, as such, general cognitive processes.

THE GUT + PERFORMANCE

Suffer from recurring infections? Often find yourself feeling a bit blue? Constantly feel like your energy has been sapped? Try giving your gut a little TLC.

+ GUT + IMMUNITY

You may be surprised to learn that 80% of the immune system is located in the gut in the form of GALT (gut associated lymphoid tissue). If you are someone who suffers from recurrent infections or increased cases of cold and the flu you may find that your gut isn't quite as happy as it should be. A compromised gut can also result in you developing allergies such as eczema, hay fever, and asthma. Not helpful when you are trying to nail that project deadline or ace a presentation. Look at supporting the balance of beneficial microbes or "good bacteria" in the gut as well as removing processed foods and including plenty of anti-inflammatory foods such as those high in omega 3s—chia seeds, flaxseeds, cold-water fish, free-range eggs, and grass-fed meats can help. You may also wish to seek out the help of a nutrition-trained professional to help diagnose any food intolerances that can also trigger immune-type reactions, as well as persistent digestive symptoms.

+ GUT + MOOD

Now here's a fascinating fact: 95% of our serotonin receptor sites, more commonly associated with being our "happy hormone," are located in the gut, as well as millions of other neurons and chemical messengers. This has massive implications for how we might consider mood disorders, such as depression, anxiety, and general mood, which will, of course, have an impact on performance. More recent and compelling research suggests that certain strains of gut microbes can produce their own neurotransmitter chemicals, including serotonin, as well as dopamine and GABA, two other important neurotransmitters. This means that bacteria can directly influence the way that we think and behave. The phrase "gut instinct" has never been so fitting!

 GUT + ENERGY

Think of the gut as the finely tuned engine in a racing car. If you want the fastest time on the track you need to put in the right fuel. The same goes for our bodies, and more specifically the gut. It is here that key energy-yielding nutrients from our food are absorbed and transported around the body to keep our tanks topped off. Poor absorption and assimilation of nutrients due to a struggling gut means we can feel fatigued and generally low in energy if we are left deficient. Probiotic microbes in the gut also have a role to play in synthesizing certain energy-supportive vitamins, such as biotin, folic acid, thiamine, B_{12}, and vitamin K. So keeping a healthy gut flora helps support energy levels, too.

PLENISH YOUR GUT

The word probiotic means "pro life," which in itself makes a very powerful statement.

➕ PROBIOTICS

In a healthy gut, probiotics are the microbes we want to flourish. Predominantly these derive from two major strains, lactobacillus and bifidobacterium. Ideally these sit nicely alongside other bacteria to provide a harmonious and perfectly balanced environment. However, in modern lifestyles, with all the extraneous factors we throw at the gut, including processed and refined foods, certain medications, and stress, many of us cultivate fewer of these "friendly" bacteria, and this is where digestive symptoms start to arise.

Having a healthy gut flora is important. Probiotics are crucial for assimilating nutrients and promoting regularity. They also switch on and manage the activity of immune-cell tissue, as well as fighting off potential pathogens, such as viruses and parasites. You could think of them as your own internal army. According to recent studies, they can also influence our mood by producing positive neurotransmitters.

The best way to support the growth of beneficial bacteria is to stick with whole foods in their most natural state and avoid refined processed foods that do nothing for your gut. Try to have plenty of fiber, through a wide choice of vegetables, since these help to feed the good guys. Prebiotic foods, such as onions, garlic, leeks, almonds, oats, bananas, and endives all help support this natural growth, too. More specifically, you can take in probiotics directly from foods that have been fermented, such as kefir, sauerkraut, cultured yogurts, miso, tempeh, kimchi, and pickles. Some strains also do well in food products aimed specifically at this, and techniques such as cold-pressing and encapsulating can ensure that the probiotic reaches its final destination intact. We should aim to have some kind of pre- or probiotic food in some form every day to keep a healthy balance in the gut.

EATING FOR A STRONG MIND + BODY

Eating consciously is something that has been lost in our fast and frantic lifestyle. Most of us eat rapidly, with multiple media devices on the go. This can have a significant effect on our digestion.

➕ MINDFUL EATING

Try to eat in a relaxed environment with no distractions. Think "rest and digest." Chew your food thoroughly, and allow yourself to be fully present with your food and your plate. It's one of the simplest and most effective practices you can do to maintain a healthy digestion every single day. You'll notice that many of our recipes have a suggested chewing time per bite. This isn't a science, but just a reminder that your stomach does not have teeth, so make sure you chew well to break down your food before it goes into the digestive tract. You may find an immediate improvement in bloating and digestive symptoms.

Learning to be mindful about which foods make you feel a certain way is very powerful knowledge. When you know you're going to need extra energy, focus, and concentration you can choose foods to give you a boost when you need it most (see overleaf).

GUT-HEALTHY FOODS

Avocado–contains healthy fats as well as being a good source of glutathione, which helps support natural detoxification and elimination processes.

Nuts–a good source of polyphenols that help bacteria produce antioxidant and anti-inflammatory substances.

Coconut oil–one of nature's best natural antimicrobials, helping support the beneficial bacteria while managing the not-so-friendly bugs.

Cultured or probiotic products–dairy or nondairy sources, such as yogurt, that provide a direct source of beneficial bacteria.

Fermented foods–unpasteurized sauerkraut, kimchi, tempeh, kefir (water and milk based), miso, and pickled ginger all contain high levels of probiotics that are generated during the fermentation process, and this supports a healthy balance of bacteria in the gut.

Broccoli, kale, cabbage–all contain glucosinolates that help switch on anti-inflammatory markers, binding onto potential pathogenic substances in the colon, and removing them from the body. They also support natural detoxification processes.

Sweet potatoes–contain fermentable fibers that help support the growth of beneficial bacteria in the gut.

Garlic and onions–allium family vegetables in their most raw state contain inulin, which is an excellent prebiotic source. Garlic is also one of the most potent natural antibiotics you can get, and helps keep a healthy balance of microbes in the gut.

Apples–contain pectin in their skin that the microbes love to eat. This supports a healthy balance of bacteria in the gut and it also helps maintain regularity.

Chia and flaxseeds–provide plant-based omega 3 oils that help support anti-inflammatory processes in the gut as well as being fiber-rich to promote regular bowel motions.

Bananas–work as a prebiotic to stimulate the growth of beneficial bacteria in the gut due to inulin, a type of resistant starch. Plus, bananas provide a source of potassium that plays an essential role in smooth muscle function, helping support the movement of the gut.

RECIPE FOR SUCCESS

In this chapter we introduce you to some proudly ambitious individuals. They reveal what drives them and the things they do to proactively fuel forward ready to dream big, reach for the stars, and crush it.

Gone are the days where the leaders of tomorrow are fueled on carbonated soft drinks, coffee, and chocolate and sleep three hours a night.

The new breed of entrepreneurs and successful leaders view their health and lifestyle as the physical and emotional foundation on which to build their success. Investments in a healthy lifestyle like food, drink, and exercise are not luxuries but essential building blocks for the business and life they want to create.

Ambition is the key common denominator of this group, and it doesn't only apply to their work. They have a drive to be successful in all areas of their very busy, very inspirational lives! Follow their lead to succeed on your own ambitious path.

THE NEW BREED OF ENTREPRENEUR

Driven by
passion

not financial
reward

100%

of the people we profiled
are proud to say they
are very ambitious

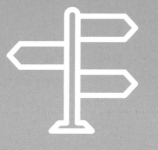

Entrepreneurs always
feel as though there is
a lot more to achieve
on their journey

Schedule exercise
as a priority

7 to 8
HOURS

Sleep on average about
7 to 8 hours a night

ARIEL FOXMAN

I met Ariel in New York in 2001. He was in his 20s and already one of the most impressive people I knew. A Harvard grad with a BA in English, Ariel had already had an editorial role at *The New Yorker*. Ariel went off in his 20s to launch and become editor of a new Condé Nast men's magazine called *Cargo*. By 34, he was named editor-in-chief of *InStyle* magazine, being the first man to helm the title. The *InStyle* and *StyleWatch* brands had a reach of more than 27 million women. Ariel oversaw the core magazine, 14 international editions, and all digital properties. Even though he's often photographed with Julia Roberts, Jennifer Aniston, Heidi Klum, and other megawatt stars, he's not one to sit on his laurels. His ambition and drive have gained recognition by Crain's, who named Foxman as one of the "40 Under 40," a group of rising stars "who will shape New York for the next 25 years," and the *Advocate* listed him as one of the "50 Most Influential LGBT People in Media." In 2011, 2012, and 2015, he was featured on *Out*'s annual Power List.

1. What is your title and what do you do? Former editorial director and editor-in-chief of *InStyle* and *StyleWatch* and the Digital InStyle Collection at Time Inc. US where I was responsible for content and strategy, digital acceleration, and new revenue streams.

2. What time do you wake up and go to sleep? I wake up between 6 and 8 a.m. and go to sleep between 10 p.m. and 1 a.m. I strive to bring routine to this aspect of my life!

3. Favorite meal of the day? Breakfast. Here, I have mastered routine! Weekdays, I pretty much always have black iced coffee, two hard-boiled eggs, and a banana. On the weekend, I brunch with my husband or friends, and while it usually involves eggs and potatoes, I am less rigid.

4. Other than work, what are you passionate about? My family. I like to spend as much as quality time with my parents and my sister and her three incredible children as I can. I love being an involved uncle. I am passionate about my marriage and my husband. I love being a part of his life, supporting his career, dreams. And I am passionate about information: I am constantly reading, scanning, downloading media.

5. How did you get started? I was the editor-in-chief of my school newspaper. And then, in college, I wrote film reviews for one of the papers. When I graduated, I leveraged a summer internship at a book publishing house into a full-time job in NYC. Once there I met an editor who had come from magazines and she introduced me to an opportunity at *Details* magazine that I nabbed and made the transition.

6. Do you consider yourself ambitious? What does ambition feel like to you? Yes. It feels like wanting to check off my to-do list with vigor but always making sure to add elements of curiosity and risk to that list—if not daily, then weekly.

7. Who or what motivates you? A dream of having a family of my own. My husband. The audience of our brands.

8. You've been in publishing for nearly 20 years. Where are you in your journey? Just getting started. I believe in multiple chapters and always being a student of life.

9. How do you get it all done? I do not. I am still getting comfortable with the fact that it's never actually done.

10. Being busy, what are your top tips for staying healthy? You have to make it a priority. Treat healthy behavior like you do the things you do for other people.

11. Top tip for being successful? Be kind. Always.

12. Your guilty pleasure? Reality TV. Diet beverages.

13. What is your go-to juice when you have a huge day and need to crush it? I love any green juice that has no fruit in it. OK to lemon.

THE ARIEL

INGREDIENTS

+ 1 cucumber
+ 2 cups spinach, tightly packed

+ 4 to 5 broccoli florets
+ ½ lemon

KARREN BRADY

As the CEO of West Ham FC, a mother of two, and survivor of brain aneurysm surgery, Baroness Brady of Knightsbridge CBE is one of the most influential, high-profile, and respected female business leaders in the UK. Voted Business Woman of the Year, Ultimate Entrepreneur, and rated among the 50 most inspirational people in the world, she is passionate about business and the promotion of women in business in the UK. Lady Brady was made a life peer by the Prime Minister, entering the House of Lords in 2014, and received a CBE from Queen Elizabeth II for her services to business, entrepreneurship, and women in business. I love her empowering attitude that although you can't determine where you start in life, you can determine where you end up.

1. What's your title and what do you do? Baroness Brady of Knightsbridge CBE. I am the CEO of West Ham Football (soccer) Club, a member of the House of Lords, the Small Business Ambassador for the Government, I appear on BBC show *The Apprentice*, and I am a global inspirational speaker.

2. What time do you wake up and go to sleep? Up at 7 a.m., in bed at 11 p.m. My staff will tell you I send the odd email at 4 a.m.!

3. Favorite meal of the day? Dinner: the only meal I ever eat.

4. Other than work, what are you passionate about? Helping other women in business, raising the importance of having women in executive positions on company boards, promoting the benefits of owning your own business, inspiring young women to be ambitious.

5. How did you get started? I left school at 18 and went straight to work at Saatchi & Saatchi. I had only three things: my ambition—my main goal was independence and I didn't want to be told what to do and when to do it by anyone; my determination—I was prepared to work hard, be dedicated, and push myself, and as a result I did not have a day off in 13 years; my integrity—having the principle of doing the right thing is at the heart of everything I do. My grandmother always told me to "never look down on people unless I am helping them up."

6. Do you consider yourself ambitious? If yes, are you proud to say that out loud? Yes, very much so. No one ever started anything without ambition. It is a shame that we tend to shy away from ambitious people; we have somehow confused being ambitious with being ruthless and nothing could be further from the truth. Bottom line is if you don't champion your career, no one will do it for you.

7. What motivates you? The toughest thing about being a success is that you have to keep on being a success, and this takes drive and ambition. Nothing is work unless you'd rather be doing something else, and other than my family there is nothing else I would rather be doing. This is why it is so important to pick a career that you love.

8. Where are you in your journey? I hope halfway through. The first few years of your career are the hardest but also the most rewarding, as you learn so much. Over the years I have adapted my life to keep learning.

9. How do you get it all done? I am a decision-maker, therefore I get things done. I am not afraid to pick up the phone and call people I do not know and ask for what I want! I employ smart people and promote great culture in my company. I am naturally curious, I don't believe I know it all, and am always looking to learn. I like what I do and therefore don't mind doing it all day, and long into the night!

10. Being busy, what are your top tips for staying healthy? I take vitamin D and drink 3 litres (3 quarts) of water every day. I only drink alcohol at weekends.

11. Top tip for being successful? When I had surgery I learned that you only get one life and you have to live it. Be the best you can be and hope to never look back and say "I wish I had…".

12. Your guilty pleasure? I have a Hydrafacial once a month and my hair done once a fortnight.

13. What is your go-to juice when you have a huge day and need to crush it? Beet and pineapple juice.

THE KARREN

INGREDIENTS
+ 3 beets
+ 2 cups pineapple

EMMA SINCLAIR

Tatler magazine described Emma as a tech head who will "be running the universe one day." She remains the youngest person to have floated a company on the London Stock Exchange, having done so at 29. She now co-leads global software company EnterpriseJungle. An SAP Partner, it was recently voted the most innovative new enterprise software company. In 2014 she became UNICEF's first Business Mentor as well as co-founding the UK's first health and well-being members' space. She truly believes entrepreneurship can change the world, and that teaching basic business skills can change the course of someone's life. I first met Emma when she interviewed me for the *Telegraph*. She is one of the sharpest, and unapologetically ambitious people I've met. When I hit a roadblock in business or health, Emma is on speed dial.

1. What is your title and what do you do? Co-founder of EnterpriseJungle. We build innovative, cloud-based enterprise software focused on talent supply: Essentially game-changing tools for large companies that give competitive advantage by intelligently leveraging big data and cloud technology.

2. What time do you wake up and go to sleep? I'm an early riser. Like many of my peers, if I want to commit to exercise, first thing is the only time I can consistently and reliably fit it in! Additionally, my co-founder is based overseas so a conversation first thing GMT suits us both.

3. Favorite meal of the day? In California, where healthy, nutritious vegan food is everywhere, every meal is my favorite! At home in London, I love a good breakfast, such as hemp milk protein shakes, tofu scramble with spinach and sun-dried tomatoes, oatmeal, or avocado on toast.

4. Other than work, what are you passionate about? Business is my hobby, not just my profession. It is this passion that has led me to have other exciting opportunities, such as becoming UNICEF's first Business Mentor in 2014. The role was a real catalyst for my love of Africa, having made a trip to Zambia in 2014 and then Malawi in 2016.

5. How did you get started? I've always had a strong work ethic: I begged my way into my first job at 16. Long before that, I was reading my father the share prices on the way to school, so the concept of equities, stock markets, and business has been part of my life since I was four or five.

6. Do you consider yourself ambitious? Yes, without question. It comes naturally to me. And when I am interested in something, I always strive to excel.

7. Who or what motivates you? My family and my desire to make them proud. My father worked tirelessly to provide me with a fantastic education and opportunities to thrive. I want to be able to offer those same opportunities to my family.

8. Where are you in your journey? I feel experienced, confident, and better placed than I ever have to face the challenges that journeys bring. When perplexing situations present themselves, I think of something a friend recently said to me: "You've got it covered: you've been in training for this your whole life." He is right.

9. How do you get it all done? Put simply—I don't. But I do the best I can with the time I have available.

10. Being busy, what are your top tips for staying healthy? I eat well, exercise, find time to breathe and decompress, both physically and mentally, and include projects and people in my life who inspire, excite, and challenge me.

11. Top tip for being successful? Success is so subjective. Happiness, peace, love, family, and being able to pay the bills are what I strive for and my measure of success.

12. Your guilty pleasure? Ketchup, salt and vinegar potato chips, questionable pop music, and romcoms. Don't tell!

13. What is your go-to juice when you have a huge day and need to crush it? Cucumber, spinach, celery, and lemon juice are my go-to green juice ingredients.

THE EMMA

INGREDIENTS

+ 1 cucumber
+ 3 cups spinach, tightly packed

+ 3 to 4 celery stalks
+ 1/2 lemon

OZWALD BOATENG

I first learned about Ozwald Boateng in my days working for *Men's Vogue* in New York. I read romantically about how he became the first tailor to show at Paris Fashion Week, had received an OBE (Order of the British Empire) from Queen Elizabeth II, and by his 40s had a retrospective of his career in fashion at the V & A Museum, in London. The fact that he regularly dresses some of the world's most stylish celebrities (think Will Smith, Richard Branson, and Jamie Foxx) was just icing on the cake. The "King of Savile Row" has transformed menswear. He's created a unique shopping experience in his luxurious flagship store, and has used his creativity and execution to start the Made in Africa foundation. He elegantly summed up his drive as enjoying the satisfaction in completion; his discipline is inspirational and palpable!

1. What's your title and what do you do? Fashion designer.

2. What time do you wake up and go to sleep? I wake up around 6 a.m. and go to bed quite late, around 1 or 2 a.m.

3. Favorite meal of the day? Definitely dinner. I rarely eat lunch.

4. Other than work, what are you passionate about? Being creative. I love making short films, love cars, but am passionate and very involved with the foundation I set up called Made in Africa. A company with the aim of creating businesses that transform the lives of Africans in terms of employment, homes, education, energy, and health. We've already brought in over $100 billion dollars in infrastructure investment.

5. How did you get started? When I was 16, I was doing a degree in computer programing. My girlfriend asked me to help her with her fashion collection for her final year project. I really enjoyed it and realized I was quite good at it. So much so, I changed my degree (much to the chagrin of my father!). I went to a famous buyer with my collection from school, and started working and selling right out of school.

6. Do you consider yourself ambitious? Yes, very. It's just a way of life.

7. Who or what motivates you? I am very motivated to make things happen. My dad told me when I was five he had very high expectations of me, and I think it set me up to always aim high and achieve. I like to see things complete, and the ambition is about the satisfaction of that completion. It's what I love about fashion, and a particular collection. Fashion is about living in the future, having a creative idea, then visualizing the fabric, and turning the fabric into a finished product. It's a similar process for my work with Made in Africa. We have the creative vision, and then figure out the finance and the physical way to build the project.

8. Where are you in your journey? Just the beginning.

9. How do you get it all done? I can multi-task. What helps me move through the projects is discipline of execution and completion. I've tried many ways over the years, and being very structured, I'm quite quick on coming up with a creative solution when a problem is presented. Then I need to block out time to execute.

10. Being busy, what are your top tips for staying healthy? Bikram yoga a few times a week. It's easy to get out of sync, especially when you travel. I find Bikram not only keeps me fit, but makes me more effective in decision-making. I have also learned to meditate to stay balanced.

11. Top tip for being successful? Find a job you love doing.

12. Your guilty pleasure? I love movies: making and watching them. I also love spicy food, particularly chile. I've sourced some of the hottest chiles from Ghana to add to my meals.

13. What is your go-to juice when you have a huge day and need to crush it? Apple, spinach, and ginger with a fiery chile kick.

THE OZWALD

INGREDIENTS

+ 2 to 3 red apples
+ 2 cups spinach, tightly packed
+ 2-inch piece fresh ginger root
+ slice of chile for extra heat

PAUL LINDLEY

If you've shopped for baby food over the last 10 years, Paul Lindley and his organic baby food business, Ella's Kitchen will need little introduction. Paul launched Ella's Kitchen in 2006 into a very competitive space, and in a short amount of time it became one of the global market leaders due to their clean, organic ingredients and the innovative squeeze pouch. Dedicated to doing good and doing well, Paul has been a driving force for promoting good nutrition for children through several charitable initiatives. After selling Ella's Kitchen in 2013, Paul has set his sights on his next venture: Paddy's Bathroom. Named after his second child, it is a range of clean, simple bathtime soaps and haircare products for kids. Each purchase made benefits clean water initiatives in Africa. Paul is one of my food industry heros!

1. What's your title and what do you do? Founder and chairman of Ella's Kitchen; founder and CEO of Paddy's Bathroom, and above all Ella and Paddy's dad. I work to show that business can and should effect positive social change.

2. What time do you wake up & go to sleep? Up at 7:30 a.m., go to sleep at midnight usually.

3. Favorite meal of the day? Evening meal—called tea in our house—when my family are all together.

4. Other than work, what are you passionate about? Food, social entrepreneurship, Africa, children's rights, and playing most sports.

5. How did you get started? I had just had my first child, Ella, and had an idea for healthy, handy, fun foods for young children that would improve their lives and develop a healthier relationship with food. I thought I'd regret it if I didn't follow through with the idea, so I handed my notice in and took two years to develop the brand and products.

6. Do you consider yourself ambitious? If yes, are you proud to say that out loud? Yes, absolutely! Ambition is a good thing! I believe we should all use our lives to do all that we can to leave the world a better place than we found it. The

trick is to keep your head in the clouds and your feet on the ground. I don't mind failing, but I really don't like setting goals that are too easy, as then you never know how much you could have achieved!

7. Who or what motivates you? My children and doing what I can to help them make the best they can of their lives and talents. I am also more motivated by internal rewards of independence, mastery, connectedness, self-confidence, and challenge than by external motivations of promotion, recognition, or bonus.

8. Where are you in your journey? On the path less trodden.

9. How do you get it all done? By not really having a good sense of time! I think much more can be done in any given timescale than can actually be done, but therefore I actually achieve more than less. I'm not very well organized, but when I'm inspired I am both creative and very focused. I believe in what George Bernard Shaw said: "Some men see things as they are and ask why. I dream things that never were and ask why not?"

10. Being busy, what are your top tips for staying healthy? The ability to press pause, rewind, and play again in everything you do is time well spent to give you perspective and energy. I get most energy when I have the autonomy to do it my way, in my time, be that at a desk or on a hillside, in the shower, or on a road bike. I try to ensure I get fresh air, healthy food, and plenty of exercise every day.

11. Top tip for being successful? Be positive. Think differently. Be tenacious. Remember perspective. Listen twice as much as you speak. Worry only about the things you can control and don't spend time or energy on the things you can't. A healthy body facilitates a healthy mind.

12. Your guilty pleasure? Tuscan red wine.

13. What is your go-to juice when you have a huge day and need to crush it? Orange, carrot, and ginger.

THE PAUL

INGREDIENTS

+ 3 oranges
+ 5 carrots
+ 1-inch piece fresh ginger root

SARAH ROBB O'HAGAN

Executive, activist, and entrepreneur, Sarah Robb O'Hagan is described by the media as everything from "Superwoman undercover" and the "Queen of the Jocks" to the ultimate example of where fierce businesswoman, mother, and fitness fanatic meet. Named among *Forbes*' "Most Powerful Women in Sports," and recognized as one of Fast Company's "Most Creative People in Business," she is an internationally recognized re-inventor of brands. But, if you ask her, she'll say she's in business to help individuals and teams achieve their potential. Sarah has had leadership roles at some of the world's most iconic brands, including Virgin and Nike, and has taken her own entrepreneurial leap to found a movement called Extreme Living, helping people unlock their potential by discovering their own exploitable traits. Yes, please!

1. What's your title and what do you do? I am an executive, an entrepreneur, and an activist.

2. What time do you wake up and go to sleep? I believe in 7 to 8 hours' sleep a night: bed by 10: 30 p.m. and up by 5:30 or 6 a.m.

3. Do you sleep well? For the most part, yes. I try to read (a book not an iPad) and that helps me fall asleep. Sometimes when I am dealing with work stress I struggle to turn my mind off. But I usually just deal with it and try to remember that everything seems easier to deal with in the light of day!

4. Favorite meal of the day? Dinner. It is the one meal I get to sit down and enjoy with my family.

5. Other than work, what are you passionate about? My family. There's nothing more fun than adventuring through life with them and watching them learn and grow. We are big travelers and adventure-seekers—it's my greatest joy to experience new things and take on challenges together. Likewise, I am energized by helping people get more out of themselves professionally and personally. That's why I started my platform ExtremeYOU.

6. How did you get started? As a marketing trainee at Air NZ. I am from New Zealand and I wanted to travel the world, so I figured Air NZ was the best place for me. I absolutely loved it. Thanks to my leaders and mentors at Air NZ, I was able to relocate to the United States and pursue my American dream.

7. Do you consider yourself ambitious? Are you proud to say that out loud? Absolutely. Yes. I have been ambitious as long as I can remember! To me it is about being an explorer. I always want to try more, see more, do more, and push myself to be more than I am today. Life is short; I don't want to get to the end and feel like I could have gotten more out of it!

8. Who or what motivates you? BIG mountains to climb (metaphorically). I love taking on challenges and testing myself. Most importantly, I love being part of a team—my family, my group of running girlfriends, or my business teams. There's nothing more fulfilling than accomplishing it together.

9. Where are you in your journey? I feel like I've got a LOOOONG way to go and so much more I want to experience.

10. How do you get it all done? I have the most incredible support system in the world. My husband is the lead parent and he totally kicks ass. He is SO organized, and thanks to him we all manage to be in the right place at the right time! Beyond that I have brilliant siblings and close friends I check in with a lot when I am trying to figure hard things out.

11. Being busy, what are your top tips for staying healthy? You MUST prioritize your health and fitness. I see my health and fitness as the foundation for everything I do. My time working out is the time each day that I make myself strong—mentally, emotionally, and physically.

12. Top tip for being successful? Get outside your comfort zone. Push yourself to find your extremes: take risks, be bold. Take ownership for all the consequences—good and bad—because that's how you grow.

13. Your guilty pleasure? Netflix!

14. What is your recipe for success? Oatmeal smoothie with blueberries and raspberries.

THE SARAH

INGREDIENTS

+ ¹/₄ cup gluten-free oats
+ ¹/₂ cup unsweetened almond or cashew
  m*lk (see page 92)

+ ¹/₂ cup blueberries
+ ¹/₃ cup raspberries

SIAN SUTHERLAND

On page 10, I talked about the entrepreneurial mantra of "Never Stand Still." Well, Sian certainly keeps moving. By 26, she had created a Michelin-starred restaurant in London, went on to create a branding agency called Miller Sutherland, and then really hit her stride when creating the global skincare brand Mama Mio for pregnant women and Mio for active women. I met Sian for a dose of inspiration, and we shared a mutual burning passion for doing good for the Earth, while doing good in business, so much so that she became an investor in Plenish and joined our journey. Her force is intangible and epic!

1. What's your title and what do you do? Chief, Insider–creating and helping build brands and businesses with soul, focusing on the wellness arena.

2. What time do you wake up and go to sleep? In a perfect world–bed by 10:30 p.m., up by 7a.m. Real world–asleep 11:30 p.m., awake 5:30 a.m., doze, up by 7 a.m.

3. Favorite meal of the day? One shared with people I love.

4. Other than work, what are you passionate about? So many things: business startups with passionate people; young entrepreneurs creating new kinds of GOOD business; society thinking less about money and more about humanity; learning new stuff; working with Plastic Oceans (plasticoceans.net) and Being Human (beinghuman.dk).

5. How did you get started? I worked in advertising until I was 25 and then left to set up my first business–crazily choosing a restaurant. Since then I have created businesses in design and brand creation, film production, and most latterly skincare.

6. Do you consider yourself ambitious? Yes. Ambitious for creating and building businesses and teams from nothing to something great. It is not about size for me, it's about the power of emotional connection with your team and your consumers. That's my measure. I am ambitious to create something that matters; I cannot just sell stuff.

7. Who or what motivates you? My mom. She is in her 90s, and works every day as a minister helping people find happiness. She's a tough act to follow and a total inspiration in how she cares about loving people whoever they are, and not about financial reward.

8. Where are you in your journey? On my second curve; trying to be patient with myself as I embark on a new phase after selling Mio and Mama Mio. As a serial entrepreneur I know the time is right for my next big thing and can't wait to get going.

9. How do you get it all done? I'd like to say I am really organized but I'm not. I am pretty good at "big picture" rather than minutiae. My gorgeous husband, Christian, is my great support, as domestic admin is not my strength. We make a top team. Workwise, I try to prioritize what is actually achieving something versus just busyness.

10. Being busy, what are your top tips for staying healthy? Exercise is essential. I hate the gym and treadmills but I love team sport, so my basketball team "The Badabings" is perfect. I started tennis lessons a few years ago and I love trying new classes when traveling. I try to meditate for 15 minutes a day outside, rain or shine. Being in nature and trying to be "in the moment" is a real 1 + 1 = 5.

11. Top tip for being successful? Success is personal and you need to have your own measures of achievement. Money and power really don't make you happy. My measure of success is having a day filled with love, laughter, joy, and that inimitable buzz that a great "achieving" day of business gives you. That's the day I feel invincible and truly lucky.

12. Your guilty pleasure? Plenish Kick laced with tequila–that's my idea of balance. And I am a firm believer in the power of minibreaks.

13. What is your go-to juice when you have a huge day and need to crush it? Chile, beet, spinach, pear, cucumber, ginger.

THE SIAN

INGREDIENTS

+ 4 beets
+ 4 cups spinach, tightly packed
+ 1 cucumber

+ 1 pear
+ 2-inch piece fresh ginger root

TAMARA HILL-NORTON

2016 marked the year that it's officially acceptable (if not chic) to wear your workout gear everywhere. The word Athleisure was inducted into the Merriam-Webster dictionary in 2016, so it's now officially a "category." Ever wonder how a global category gets started? Look no further than Tamara Hill-Norton, founder and creative officer of Sweaty Betty. Tamara and her husband Simon have inspired me to think about my brand past the initial phase, and are role models for keeping a brand identity tight and true to its core, even as it grows exponentially.

1. What's your title and what do you do? I am the chief creative officer, responsible for product and brand at Sweaty Betty.

2. What time do you wake up and go to sleep? I wake up at 7 and go to sleep at 11.

3. Favorite meal of the day? Favorite meal is dinner during the week, as we try to sit down as a family whenever we can together. But I love to cook more experimentally on weekends, using fresh vegetables from the garden. Weekend breakfasts are also top of my list, as Simon gets up to do them (letting me sleep in) and will make us amazing pancakes with buckwheat and spelt flour, flaxseeds, etc., (which our youngest son ruins by slathering in Nutella and cream while our eldest daughter tries to make up for his evil by chopping avocado on top of hers!). Simon squeezes us fresh juices, too.

4. Other than work, what are you passionate about? I am passionate about fitness, leading a healthy, but balanced lifestyle with my family, travel . . . oh, and cocktails (I have all the cocktail paraphernalia, recipe books, a beautiful cocktail trolley, and grow herbs on the windowsill as ingredients).

5. How did you get started? I was made redundant from my first job, so wrote a business plan with my husband for a concept I was passionate about and went from there.

6. Do you consider yourself ambitious? Yes, I'm ambitious. But I'm ambitious about creating a lifestyle that is balanced and fulfilled. That includes business success but not at the expense of lifestyle.

7. Who or what motivates you? Always striving to do something better than before.

8. Where are you in your journey? I'm a mother and creator of teenage children and a teenage business. It's now about direction, letting go when necessary, and providing a stable foundation and inspiring force for both.

9. How do you get it all done? By prioritizing the most important things and letting other things go, by having amazing people at work and home—whom I can trust completely—and doing some sort of exercise/activity each day for myself and my peace of mind.

10. Being busy, what are your top tips for staying healthy? Make time to exercise, build it into your daily routine so that it becomes a normal routine (like cycling to work, which I do every day). Make a point of eating good, nutritious food whenever possible. When traveling, I take my sneakers so I can run anywhere I go, and I take our travel yoga mat and follow the app yogaglo. I also take homemade protein balls and nuts for snacking.

11. Top tip for being successful? Be passionate about your work and focused on your vision/end goal.

12. Your guilty pleasure? Margarita with chile salt or Negroni—hard to choose.

13. What is your go-to juice when you have a huge day and need to crush it? Orange, grapefruit, fennel, and ginger.

THE TAMARA

INGREDIENTS

+ 1 regular or pink grapefruit, skin removed
+ 1 orange, skin removed
+ 1 whole bulb of fennel, quartered
+ 2-inch piece fresh ginger root

ZANNA VAN DIJK

Zanna Van Dijk is a blogger, vlogger, and social media fanatic. She has organically built up a substantial social media following that has allowed her to travel the world and work with brands such as Nike, NutriBullet, Nissan, and Plenish. Zanna is the author of *Strong: Your ultimate guide to achieving a fit, healthy, and balanced body*, she launched the #girlgains movement and created her own Activewear collection. I met Zanna when we featured her on the Plenish blog about rising stars in the fitness industry. I was immediately blown away by her integrity, palpable drive, and infectious positivity, as well as the commitment to fueling her own drive with a healthy eating and fitness regime that allowed her to continue to inspire others.

1. What's your title and what do you do? Personal trainer, fitness blogger, and co-founder of #girlgains, a movement which aims to unite women and inspire them to become fitter, healthier, and happier.

2. Are you an early bird or late bird? If I wake up later than 6 a.m. I consider it sleeping in! I go to bed at about 10 p.m.

3. Favorite meal of the day? Brunch is my favorite meal ever. Sometimes it's sweet, sometimes savory.

4. Other than work, what are you passionate about? Empowering people to use fitness and food to nourish and care for their bodies. I love showing people how being healthy can be fun, enjoyable, and sustainable!

5. How did you get started? I was studying speech and language therapy at university but started reading about fitness and nutrition on the side. I created an Instagram account to share recipes and meal ideas. By the time I finished university I had 30,000 followers. After traveling and spending some time thinking about my career, I decided to take a risk and ride the social media wave. I created a blog, stayed in an Air BnB in London, and did a personal training course for six weeks. I never left. I immediately started training clients every day, taking nutrition workshops, and working on my blog between clients. As the social media following grew, the personal training time reduced. I now PT once a week and work on other projects six days a week (no days off here yet!).

6. Do you consider yourself ambitious? Extremely. I am constantly internally motivated to work hard to achieve my goals and dreams! I celebrate being driven.

7. Who or what motivates you? I am very self-motivated. I find having my own goals and dreams clear in my mind is enough motivation for me to work my socks off. I have always been a hard worker regardless of what it's for. My mom describes me as a "workaholic." I'm not looking for monetary rewards or accolades from others, but to meet my own high standards.

8. Where are you in your journey? I am only at the beginning and I'm aware that I have a long way to go. I'm continuously learning about the wellness industry and about business in general and am excited for the future.

9. How do you get it all done? Lists, spreadsheets, and timetables. My life is organized to an extreme—it has to be, otherwise nothing would get done on time.

10. Being busy, what are your tops tips for staying healthy? Schedule workouts in your diary like they are a doctor's appointment, and keep them high on your priority list. I find fitting them in first thing in the morning makes sure they are complete before other distractions creep in.

11. Top tip for being successful? Stay true to yourself and stay grounded. Success can very easily go to your head. Staying humble is a challenge but it's something you should strive to do.

12. Your guilty pleasure? White chocolate.

13. What is your go-to juice when you have a huge day and need to crush it? Pineapple, spinach, cucumber, and ginger, what I call "Zanna's Pineapple Zinger"!

THE ZANNA

INGREDIENTS

+ 2 cups pineapple
+ 2 cups spinach, tightly packed

+ 1 cucumber
+ 2-inch piece fresh ginger root

4. THE JUICES

JUICING ROCKS

According to the World Health Organization, 2.7 million deaths would be avoided annually worldwide if everyone ate 14 ounces of fruit and vegetables a day. Various governments advise consuming five portions of fruit and vegetables a day, but most nutritional therapists say that is a bare minimum. Technology has advanced the pace that we all live and work at. Yet even though we have all these new demands we are still in the same bodies our ancestors lived in. This new pace demands more intelligent and efficient fuel. By consuming a glass of juice that is high in nutrient density, but low in sugar due to minimal fruit, you can easily assimilate those nutrients. You know what we say, press on—then crush it!

➕ BUT WHAT ABOUT THE FIBER?

The most common question we get on juicing is: don't I need the fiber? Fiber is an essential part of a healthy diet, but aim to get it in ways other than your juice. Fiber, by design, slows down the absorption of nutrients. By removing the soluble fiber through the juicing process, you provide your body with a hit of nutrients that are readily available to your cells and can give you energy. Keeping fruit levels low and vegetable content high, you deliver oxygen-rich goodness to your body, not sugar. Given that stress levels, poor diet, and fast-paced lives challenge your gut on a daily basis, juices allow your digestive system the chance to take a break. The recipe is key!

WHY ORGANIC?

At Plenish, we work very closely with the Soil Association, the UK's governing body on Organic. We source our raw materials exclusively from organic growers and farmers, to ensure that the integrity of the product we sell is at its highest in terms of nutrition and taste and that our growers don't use harmful pesticides.

REDUCE YOUR EXPOSURE TO POTENTIALLY HARMFUL PESTICIDES

Over 320 pesticides can be routinely used in non-organic farming and these are often present in non-organic food. Given that you press more than 2 pounds of produce into each glass of juice, we want to make sure you are pressing goodness, not pesticides!

KNOW WHAT'S IN YOUR FOOD

Here in the UK, all organic farms and food companies are inspected at least once a year and then standards for organic food are laid down in European law.

HELP COMBAT CLIMATE CHANGE

If organic farming was common practice here in the UK, for example, we could offset at least 23% of UK agriculture's greenhouse gas emissions through soil carbon sequestration alone!

HELP PROTECT OUR WILDLIFE

Research has shown that plant, insect, and bird life is 50% more abundant on organic farms and there are 30% more species.

SUPPORT HIGHER STANDARDS OF ANIMAL WELFARE

Organic animals are truly free-range. This means healthy, happy animals that are reared without the routine use of antibiotics, which is common in intensive livestock farming.

64 ➕ DIRTY DOZEN + CLEAN FIFTEEN

Not all non-organic fruits and vegetables have a high pesticide level. Some have a natural protective layer that offers a defense against sprayed pesticides. If a fruit or vegetable has a thin skin (like a berry or apple), where you eat its outer layer, you will also be ingesting the chemicals that were sprayed on. When eating something like an avocado or banana, the outer layer is discarded, so the inside has, to an extent, been protected. Every year, the Environmental Working Group (EWG)* publishes a list of the best and worst contenders. Given that organic produce can sometimes be more expensive and harder to find, this list can help you prioritize what you buy.

THE DIRTY DOZEN

Try to buy these organic:

1. Leafy greens like spinach and kale
   (the worst culprits)
2. Strawberries
3. Apples
4. Nectarines
5. Peaches
6. Celery
7. Grapes
8. Cherries
9. Spinach
10. Tomatoes
11. Bell peppers
12. Cucumbers

THE CLEAN FIFTEEN

Less of a priority to buy organic:

1. Avocado
2. Corn
3. Pineapple
4. Cabbage
5. Frozen peas
6. Onions
7. Asparagus
8. Mango
9. Papaya
10. Kiwi
11. Eggplant
12. Honeydew melon
13. Grapefruit
14. Muskmelon
15. Cauliflower

* EWG's 2016 Shopper's Guide to Pesticides in Produce™

LET'S GET JUICING

Ready to get your juice on? We know you won't want to settle for anything less than perfect, so these pointers will ensure you get the best results possible.

➕ TIPS FROM THE JUICING KITCHEN

Get prepped
Wash and prepare all of your ingredients before juicing.

Dry then wet
Always juice leafy greens and herbs first, followed by juicy fruits or water-based vegetables to wash through the bits. To yield more juice from leafy greens try running them through the juicer twice.

Slow and steady wins the race
Make sure you cut up your produce to fit the "mouth" of your juicer. If you get too greedy and try and shove it all in, the juicer will jam. Promise.

Mix it up
Stir in any spices after juicing the other ingredients.

When in doubt, add vegetables
Due to variations in fruit sizes, the serving may make a bit more or less than 2 cups (16 fl oz). If you need to bulk up a recipe, always try adding more cucumber, zucchini, or lettuce—all low in sugar but high in vitamin-infused water content.

1 cup = tightly packed
So squish that spinach or parsley down. I use a standard measuring cup, but you can use a bowl or mug of the same capacity (8 fl oz or ½ pint).

Juice recipes all make 2 cups (16 fl oz), unless otherwise stated.

FRUITLESS

FIT

Yellow bell peppers are actually very sweet, and a great source of beta-carotene, essential vitamins, and minerals, and are low in natural sugars. It's great to be able to enjoy a slightly sweet juice without the sugar. This green juice is very light and hydrating, due to the zucchini and cucumber, and has a nice, balanced fresh taste. Spinach and kale are rich in antioxidants that help protect the brain from free radicals, as well as being an excellent source of B vitamins that help reduce cognitive decline so you can stay fighting fit.

INGREDIENTS

+ 2 zucchini, trimmed, skin on
+ 1 cucumber, trimmed, skin on
+ 2 cups spinach
+ 2 cups kale
+ 1 yellow bell pepper, stalk and seeds removed

DEEP

Broccoli is an excellent source of B vitamins as well as vitamin K, which is a great anti-inflammatory agent. Great for cognitive performance and gut health. This has an unapologetic green taste, with a hint of freshness from the mint. If you're not feeling that hard core (but you want this hard core vitamin hit), you can squeeze some lime in for a bit of extra zing.

INGREDIENTS

+ 8 broccoli florets
+ 1 cucumber, trimmed, skin on
+ 4 celery stalks
+ 2 cups spinach
+ 1 cup mint

GREENS

DETOX

Fennel has long been used for liver and detoxification support. The aniseed flavor of the fennel is balanced out by the tang of the green apple and kiwi. A good juice for "the morning after the night before," when you have to act sharp, though you are feeling anything but.

INGREDIENTS

+ 1 $\frac{1}{2}$ heads of fennel
+ 1 $\frac{1}{2}$ green apples, stalk removed, skin on
+ 1 $\frac{1}{2}$ kiwis, trimmed, skin on
+ 2 cups kale

SMART

Cilantro adds a lovely fragrant taste to this slightly sweet and smart green juice.

INGREDIENTS

+ 2 cups spinach
+ 1 zucchini, trimmed, skin on
+ 1 pear, stalk removed, skin on
+ $\frac{1}{2}$ cup cilantro
+ 1 green bell pepper, seeds and stalk removed

SING

This is one of those flavor combinations that makes you want to sing! The vibrant pineapple mixed with the green chile and leafy greens is delicious and full of goodness. This juice holds up particularly well if you want to make a bigger batch and drink it for the next three days.

INGREDIENTS

+ 2 cups pineapple, skin removed
+ 1 1/2 green chiles, seeds removed
+ 1 green bell pepper, stalk and seeds removed
+ 3 cups spinach

+ 1 lime, skin on
+ 4 celery stalks
+ 8 broccoli florets

FRESH

This mild green juice has a hint of freshness from the mint and subtle sweetness from the pear. You'll feel fresh and focused to press on and crush it!

INGREDIENTS

+ 6 broccoli florets
+ 1/2 cup mint
+ 1 cucumber, trimmed, skin on

+ 1 pear, stalk removed, skin on
+ 2 cups spinach

FOCUS

Full of intelligent greens like spinach, kale, and romaine lettuce, this tart green juice is a great one for a day that needs intense focus.

INGREDIENTS

+ 1 zucchini, trimmed, skin on
+ 1 head of romaine lettuce
+ 2 cups spinach
+ 2 cups kale

+ 1 1/2 green apples, stalk removed, skin on
+ 1 lime, skin on
+ 1 lemon, pith and skin removed

BALANCE

This juice has a light and fresh taste despite very green ingredients. Fennel is great for supporting detoxification pathways, and the greens deliver a clever assortment of vital vitamins and nutrients. Apples contain pectin in their skin that microbes love to eat. This supports a healthy balance of bacteria in the gut and it also helps to maintain regularity.

INGREDIENTS

+ 1 head of fennel
+ 1 zucchini, trimmed, skin on
+ 1 green bell pepper, stalk and seeds removed
+ 1 green apple, stalk removed, skin on
+ 6 broccoli florets
+ 2 celery stalks

STRENGTH

Just $3^1/_2$ ounces (about 1 cup) of Brussels sprouts provides more than 140% of the recommended daily amount of vitamin C. Spinach is a great source of magnesium, which helps support the nervous system for a calmer mood while also maintaining consistent energy levels. This is a very balanced juice for the level of greens that get crammed in. The lemon, parsley, and ginger lift the greens for a fresh, uplifting taste so you have strength to take on the day.

INGREDIENTS

+ 3 cups Brussels sprouts (if out of season, defrost from frozen ahead of juicing)
+ 2 cups spinach
+ 1 $^1/_2$ apples, stalk removed, skin on
+ $^1/_2$ cucumber, trimmed, skin on
+ $^1/_2$ cup parsley
+ $^1/_2$ lemon, skin and pith removed
+ 1-inch piece fresh ginger root

FLIRT

This very light green juice has a subtle sweetness from the plum. You'll be ready to flirt with your next big challenge.

INGREDIENTS

+ 1 head of baby gem lettuce (or half a small head of romaine)
+ 1 cucumber

+ 1 plum, stone removed
+ $\frac{1}{4}$ lime, skin and pith on

FRUITS

TART

The sweetness from the carrots and pear, combined with tart grapefruit and a ginger kick, is delicious. I love this juice in winter, when the days are dark—the color and vitamin composition will catapult you into gear.

INGREDIENTS

+ 2 pink grapefruit, skin and pith removed
+ 2 carrots, trimmed, skin on
+ 1 pear, stalk removed, skin on
+ 2-inch piece fresh ginger root

FESTIVE

This merry juice started as a post-Christmas creation when there were extra cranberries and Christmas ingredients around. It's a great juice after a day of overeating, when your digestion feels sluggish and you need to get back into the festive swing.

INGREDIENTS

+ 1 orange, skin and pith removed
+ 1 1/2 cups cranberries (if out of season, defrost from frozen ahead of juicing)
+ 1 1/2 apples, stalk removed, skin on

+ 1 carrot, trimmed, skin on
+ pinch of ground cinnamon
+ pinch of ground nutmeg
+ 1/2 teaspoon ground flaxseeds

ZING

The lime and orange deliver a vitamin C hit and turmeric is brilliant for it's anti-inflammatory properties. Once you taste it, you'll know why we named it ZING!

INGREDIENTS

+ 2 oranges, skin and pith removed
+ 1 lime, skin removed
+ 2 carrots, trimmed, skin on

+ 1 cucumber, trimmed, skin on
+ 1 chile, seeds left in
+ thumb-sized piece fresh turmeric

ROOTS

MOTIVATE

Beets contain one of the necessary elements essential for dopamine production. Dopamine is one of our feel-good neurotransmitters. The nitric oxide also contained in beets supports better blood flow, which maintains sharper concentration and focus. Feel free to switch the beet:apple ratio if you're gung ho about beets! Always drink beet juice slowly, and chew it, as it's quite potent.

INGREDIENTS

+ 1 beet, scrubbed well, skin on
+ 3 green apples, stalk removed, skin on
+ 2-inch piece fresh ginger root

+ 4 celery stalks
+ 1 lemon, skin and pith removed

MOVE

Sweet potato and papaya meet in digestion heaven. Sweet potatoes contain fermentable fibers that help support the growth of beneficial bacteria in the gut, whereas papaya contains a proteolytic enzyme called papain, which is at its highest when the fruit is ripe and aids in protein digestion. This has a subtly sweet flavor layered with all the anti-inflammatory spices. Stir in the turmeric after juicing the other ingredients.

INGREDIENTS
+ 1 sweet potato, trimmed, scrubbed well, skin on
+ $1/2$ papaya, seeds and skin removed
+ 2 carrots, trimmed, skin on
+ 2-inch piece fresh ginger root
+ 1 orange, skin and pith removed
+ $1/4$ teaspoon ground turmeric

WARM

Another great winter warmer—it has a rich and warming seasonal flavor. Stir in the cinnamon after juicing the other ingredients.

INGREDIENTS
+ 1 parsnip, trimmed, scrubbed well, skin on
+ 1 orange, skin and pith removed
+ $11/2$ carrots, trimmed, skin on
+ $11/2$ apples, stalk removed, skin on
+ 1 cup cranberries (if out of season defrost from frozen before juicing)
+ 1-inch piece fresh ginger root
+ pinch of ground cinnamon

83

SHOTS + TONICS

PEAK

I stayed at Bronte Beach in Sydney, and the local juice bar was frequented by all the surfers. They would pick up a ginger and oil of oregano shot before or after they hit the surf to warm up. I make my own version, using fresh oregano, if I'm feeling a sore throat coming on and know I have a big day ahead. The ginger and oregano are both known for their antibacterial and warming properties, and, combined with the vitamin C from the lemon, make you feel like you can handle any wave! Makes 2¼ fl oz (about 2 x 1 fl oz shots).

INGREDIENTS

+ 5-inch piece fresh ginger root
+ ½ lemon, skin and pith removed

+ 3 sprigs of oregano, leaves only

DEFEND

A citrusy fireball of a shot. The mixture of ginger and cayenne wakes up every cell in your body. Makes 2¼ fl oz (about 2 x 1 fl oz shots).

INGREDIENTS

+ ½ orange, skin and pith removed
+ ½ lemon, skin and pith removed
+ 2-inch piece fresh ginger root

+ dash of cayenne pepper (I put in a generous pinch, but adjust depending on your love of or aversion for this spice)

SPARKLE

I wanted to create my own version of a healthy drink with a sparkly mouthfeel, similar to an effervescent vitamin tablet. This juice contains the superfood turmeric, which has great anti-inflammatory properties (try to find the fresh root, available in many grocery stores or Asian supermarkets). You can make a few batches of this juice and top it off with sparkling water throughout the day. Juicing turmeric can leave a yellow stain, so wear rubber gloves and be careful of clothing (or nicely manicured nails). Makes 1 cup.

INGREDIENTS

+ 4-inch piece fresh ginger root
+ 1-inch piece fresh turmeric

+ 1 small green apple
+ ½ cup sparkling water

NUT M*LKS

In case you're not on the nut m*lk wagon yet, we thought we'd give you a few good reasons to get on board.

➕ GOOD FOR YOUR SKIN

Physicians aren't just recommending the milk substitute for the lactose intolerant. They also recommend it to acne sufferers, as it's free of the hormones present in dairy and soy milk. Some nutritionists say almond milk also edges soy milk in having less fat and fewer carbohydrates and calories, but more calcium. In *Reverse the Signs of Aging*, by Dr. Nigma Talib (skin doctor to the stars), she devotes a chapter to what she calls "Dairy Face." Common symptoms of consuming too much dairy include swollen eyelids, dark circles, white bumps, and chin spots, which is why she recommends eliminating dairy from your diet.

➕ GOOD FOR WEIGHT LOSS

Nut m*lk may appeal to people trying to lose weight, as it typically contains fewer calories than skim milk—around 60 per serving. That is about 50% less than cow's milk, plus it has no cholesterol.

➕ GOOD FOR YOUR BRAIN

All nuts contain vitamin E, a potent antioxidant that helps prevent cognitive damage, keeping your brain sharp.

➕ YOU WON'T MISS THE CALCIUM

Cow's milk has the reputation of being an amazing calcium source for strong bones, but nothing could be further from the truth. The protein in cow's milk creates an acidic environment in your bloodstream that ends up robbing calcium FROM your bones and making you more prone to osteoporosis. Try increasing your intake of plant-based calcium sources like dark leafy greens (see the green juice recipes on pages 66-74), lentils, and almonds. Combine these with coconut oil or extra virgin olive oil to help your body absorb vitamins K and D (which also support strong bones). Just one cup of broccoli or chard can provide more than half the recommended daily amount of calcium.

➕ BETTER FOR COWS, BETTER FOR THE ENVIRONMENT

OK, we went there. But think about it, a cow has to be pregnant at some point so that she starts producing milk. This leads to a pretty dreadful chain of animal exploitation and disease. A 9-ounce glass of cow's milk is full of hormones that are meant for a calf to grow exponentially in the first few months of life. All those hormones, among them estrogen, testosterone, and insulin growth factor, affect your body tremendously. These hormones can interfere with your own hormones, cause you to gain weight, have mood swings, or acne.

➕ EASY TO PREPARE

Each of the following nut m*lk recipes makes 2 to 2½ cups of thick (smoothie-like) nut m*lk. Preparing them couldn't be easier. Simpy blend all the ingredients until smooth (around 2 minutes). Let stand to settle for a couple of minutes, then strain through cheesecloth or a fine strainer. (Wetting the cheesecloth will help it stick to the sides of the jar or cup and avoid spillage.) Depending on the speed of your blender you might need to do this process twice to end up with a smooth m*lk. Chill before drinking, and add more water if you like a thinner consistency.

WALNUT COFFEE

As well as vitamin E, walnuts also contain omega 3, which is linked to improved brain functioning. Walnut m*lk on its own can be somewhat bitter, so we've come up with these three delicious, creamy creations.

INGREDIENTS

+ 1 $^1/_2$ cups walnuts, soaked in water for 4 hours and drained
+ 1 shot of coffee, cooled
+ 2 $^1/_2$ cups water
+ 2 dates

MALTED WALNUT

INGREDIENTS

+ 1 $^1/_2$ cups walnuts soaked in water for 4 hours and drained
+ 2 $^1/_2$ cups water
+ 1 date
+ $^1/_2$ teaspoon ground cinnamon
+ splash of vanilla extract
+ 1 teaspoon maca powder

MATCHA WALNUT

INGREDIENTS

+ 1 $^1/_2$ cups walnuts, soaked in water for 4 hours and drained
+ 2 $^1/_2$ cups water
+ 1 date
+ $^1/_2$ teaspoon matcha green tea

HAZELNUT

For the purists among you, follow this recipe for pure, unadulterated hazelnut milk. If you like something a little more decadent, try the chocolate version below.

INGREDIENTS

+ 1 $\frac{1}{2}$ cups hazelnuts, soaked in water for at least 4 hours and drained

+ 3 cups water
+ pinch of Himalayan salt

CHOCOLATE HAZELNUT

If you were to ask me for any guilty pleasure, it would be covered in Nutella. Make sure you use a good-quality cacao, since this determines the level of deliciousness. If it's old or cheap, it can just taste a little dusty instead of decadent and chocolatey.

INGREDIENTS

+ 1 $\frac{1}{2}$ cups hazelnuts, soaked in water for at least 4 hours and drained
+ 3 cups water

+ 3 teaspoons cacao powder
+ 3 dates
+ pinch of Himalayan salt

BRAZIL NUT M*LK

In addition to vitamin E, brazil nuts contain selenium, a trace mineral essential to normal immune function. This is a very satisfying m*lk due to the high monounsaturated fats that naturally occur in brazil nuts. A great post-workout snack when you need to maintain your energy levels for the next challenge.

INGREDIENTS
+ 1 cup brazil nuts, soaked in water for at least 4 hours and drained
+ 2 $\frac{1}{2}$ cups water
+ generous pinch of ground cinnamon
+ 2 dates
+ pinch of ground nutmeg
+ pinch of Himalayan salt

ALMOND NUT M*LK

Soak the almonds in the water overnight, then blend until smooth. Pass through cheesecloth and squeeze out all the liquid, discarding the pulp. Vanilla, dates, and Himalayan sea salt are ultra delish if you want to add some flavoring.

INGREDIENTS
+ $^3/_4$ cup almonds
+ 1 $^3/_4$ cups water

CASHEW M*LK

Soak the cashews in the water for at least 2 hours, then blend until smooth. We like our cashew m*lk quite creamy but for more of a skim-milk consistency, run the blended mixture through a cheesecloth to remove the pulp.

INGREDIENTS
+ $^3/_4$ cup cashews
+ 1 $^3/_4$ cups water

COLD BREW COFFEE

WAKE

This cold brew coffee is insanely delicious with any of the nut m*lks in this book, so we just had to include it.

Ever wondered what the fuss is about cold-brewed coffee? Well, here are your alternatives: pouring hot coffee over ice—problem? It waters it down. Chilling hot coffee—marginally better, but you lose that lovely coffee aroma that's a big part of the sensory experience. Cold brewing is the proper way to enjoy an iced coffee, and the flavor is sweeter and less acidic than hot brewed coffee.

This isn't technically a juice but, let's be honest, it is very hard to replicate the jolt that coffee delivers in our most needy moments. Besides, one cup of high-quality organic coffee can be a good source of antioxidants.

Caffeinated drinks can increase acid levels in the stomach, resulting in heartburn or bloating, so limit yourself to one cup and consume in the morning, so as not to affect your evening sleep.

INGREDIENTS

+ coarsely ground coffee, ideally organic and Fairtrade certified (if you are grinding beans yourself, use a medium setting; the grind has to be coarse enough to be filtered by the mesh filter in your French press)
+ ½ cup cold water (or, if making a bigger batch, just follow a 3:1 coffee to water ratio)

Optional:
+ pinch of ground cinnamon
+ sea salt flakes
+ nut m*lk of your choice (see pages 86–92)

Add coffee and water to your French press and stir. Put on the lid with the plunger up (do not push down).

Put the un-plunged press in the fridge and let stand for 12 to 24 hours.

Plunge to separate the coffee from the grounds. Drink straight up, or pour over ice. Stir in a pinch of cinnamon, sea salt to taste, and a dash of nut m*lk, if liked.

5. THE FOOD

JOSEPHINE O'HARE

Josephine is highly commended from the Ballymaloe Cookery School, and has an FdSc in Culinary Arts from Westminster Kingsway College. She's worked in Michelin-starred London restaurants and private homes across the UK and abroad.

Josephine's cooking is "veg-centric" and mindful: her philosophy is to use fresh seasonal vegetables aplenty, and free-range, organic meat and fish in moderation, both for one's well-being, and in consideration of the environment. She believes that a chef's job doesn't end when the plate is wiped clean. Naturally, food should look appetizing and taste amazing in the moment, but that positivity should be lasting. How food makes you feel afterward is key for Josephine, thus her cooking makes abundant use of fresh, whole produce and avoids overly refined or processed ingredients.

THE FOOD

- Ⓟ PALEO
- ⓢⒻ REFINED SUGAR FREE
- Ⓖ GLUTEN FREE
- Ⓓ DAIRY FREE
- Ⓥ VEGETARIAN + VEGAN

The role of a chef is quite intimate. The food a chef creates is ingested by you, and creates building blocks for brand new cells. One might say that you should be as choosy about your food and who makes it as you are about your lovers!

I am a massive fan of Josephine O'Hare's "veg-centric" approach to cooking. It wasn't until we met in person at a Plenish event that I felt her palpable passion and ambition to create food that not only evokes pleasure when eating it, but respects the responsibility and intimacy of creating food that affects the way we feel, look, and act for days and years to come. The menu opposite started around a table with Eve (see page 24), Josephine, and me—and the lists of gut- and brain-healthy foods on pages 30–31 and 36–37 that are designed to help you achieve 110%. These recipes have been expertly created and deliciousness tested, so make sure to savor each bite and chew, chew, chew!

 # CHEW

We're about to present some delicious, gut-friendly, brain-healthy meals. Slow down and savor every bite.

➕ PRACTICING MINDFUL EATING

We sometimes spend so much time preparing our food, making it look beautiful, or Instagram worthy, but then scoff it down while reading emails or watching TV. Chewing slowly and thoroughly isn't just good manners—it also allows the enzymes in our saliva to begin breaking down our food, starting the digestive process.

Turn off the TV, leave your phone in the other room, and savor your meal. By practicing this, you are already bringing your body into a "rest and digest" state where you absorb the nutrients from the food you've carefully prepared. Try following our chewing guide per mouthful as a small challenge. It may seem awkward at first, but notice if you feel more satisfied with less food and less bloated after eating.

MENU

BREAKFAST

DINNER + LUNCHTIME

SNACKS

98

SPICED CARROT + WALNUT BREAKFAST LOAF WITH ORANGE + TURMERIC

 P **G** **D** **SF**

This loaf is just awesome. It's perfect for a quick breakfast, but fabulous as a snack, too. The psyllium husk isn't a deal-breaker. It helps bind the loaf together in the absence of gluten. The recipe will work without it, and the loaf will simply have a softer texture.

MAKES APPROXIMATELY 8 SLICES

APPROXIMATELY 40 CHEWS PER MOUTHFUL

DRY INGREDIENTS

+ 2 cups ground almonds (or just 1 1/2 cups if using fine almond flour)
+ 1 tablespoon psyllium husk
+ 1 teaspoon baking powder
+ 1/2 cup coconut palm sugar
+ pinch of salt
+ generous pinch of ground cinnamon
+ generous pinch of ground ginger
+ generous pinch of ground turmeric
+ freshly grated nutmeg
+ 1/3 cup golden raisins

+ 1/3 cup walnuts
+ 2 tablespoons flaxseeds, or ground flaxseeds

WET INGREDIENTS

+ 3 organic carrots, peeled and grated
+ 1 ripe banana, mashed or blended
+ 2 eggs
+ 1 cup mild cold-pressed organic canola oil or melted coconut oil
+ 1 teaspoon vanilla extract
+ zest of 1 orange

Preheat the oven to 400°F, and line a loaf pan with nonstick parchment paper.

Measure all the dry ingredients into a large mixing bowl, sifting in the baking powder and the coconut palm sugar to break up any lumps.

In another bowl or large pitcher, beat the carrot and banana with the rest of the wet ingredients.

Pour the beaten wet ingredients into the dry ingredients. Stir to combine.

Spoon into the lined loaf pan and bake in the oven for 25 minutes. Turn the oven down to 350°F and continue cooking for a further

35 minutes. The loaf is ready when the top is firm to the touch, and a skewer inserted into the middle comes out clean.

Let cool in the pan for a few minutes, then gently invert onto a cooling rack. Let cool completely before slicing.

The loaf will keep for 4 days sealed in an airtight container at room temperature and is best kept whole and sliced as needed. Wholesome, not too sweet, and totally, totally delicious!

BAKED EGGS WITH MUSHROOMS, SPINACH, GOAT CHEESE + CHILE

This is a weekend brunch must! It's very straightforward to prepare, yet offers something a little bit different and the pumpkin seeds add a wonderful crunch. If you fancy something more substantial, a layer of cooked quinoa in the bottom of the oven dish works well, and beautifully absorbs the rich mushroom and spinach juices.

⊕ SERVES 2

👄 APPROXIMATELY 35 CHEWS PER MOUTHFUL

INGREDIENTS

+ 2 portobello mushrooms
+ 1 tablespoon extra virgin olive oil or cold-pressed organic canola oil
+ 1 packed cup baby spinach
+ freshly grated nutmeg
+ 1 teaspoon Dijon mustard
+ 2 tablespoons crumbled goat cheese

+ 3 large eggs
+ 1 tablespoon pumpkin seeds
+ 1 teaspoon dried red chile flakes
+ 1 lemon
+ few sprigs of fresh thyme (optional)
+ salt and pepper

Preheat the oven to 400°F and place an oven rack near the top.

Wipe the mushrooms clean, and slice. Heat the oil in a medium saucepan. When hot, add the mushrooms and sauté. Season with salt and pepper. Keep the heat high, as this will encourage the water released from the mushrooms to evaporate and prevent the overall dish from being soggy.

After 5 minutes add the spinach, some freshly grated nutmeg, and the Dijon mustard and stir. Once the spinach has wilted, turn off the heat.

Scatter the mushroom and spinach mixture into a small ovenproof dish. Crumble the goat cheese evenly over the surface and crack the three eggs on top. Scatter with the pumpkin seeds and add a grinding of black pepper. Then sprinkle with the chile flakes.

Bake at the top of the oven for 10 minutes, or until the whites of the eggs are set, but the yolk remains slightly runny (or as you like it).

Let rest for a few minutes, then squeeze over some fresh lemon juice and serve in shallow bowls. A scattering of thyme leaves is a lovely addition if you have any on hand.

This dish should be juicy and creamy; wholesome comfort food perfect for kick-starting an active Saturday morning!

BANANA + BLUEBERRY PANCAKES

 P G D SF V

These pancakes are absolutely brilliant for a lazy weekend morning. They are light and fluffy in texture, and yet set you up for the day perfectly. They are also dead easy to make!

➕ MAKES 8 TO 10 PANCAKES

👄 APPROXIMATELY 15 CHEWS PER MOUTHFUL

INGREDIENTS
+ 1 ripe banana
+ 2 eggs
+ ½ cup ground almonds
+ 1 tablespoon psyllium husk
+ 1 teaspoon baking soda
+ pinch of ground cinnamon
+ pinch of salt
+ ¼ cup Plenish almond m*lk
+ few drops of vanilla extract
+ ½ cup blueberries
+ 2 tablespoons coconut oil, for cooking

OPTIONAL TOPPINGS
+ coconut yogurt
+ fresh orange, sliced
+ maple syrup or honey
+ toasted nuts and seeds

Place all of the ingredients except the blueberries and oil into a large mixing bowl. Blend well using a hand blender. A jug blender, a potato masher, or a whisk will also work. Once blended, stir in the blueberries.

Heat the coconut oil in a large skillet, just a tablespoon at a time, over medium heat. Dollop the pancake batter into the hot skillet; I find about 3 pancakes at a time works well but it depends on the size of your skillet. Let them cook for 3 to 4 minutes on the first side before flipping over and cooking for 2 minutes on the second side. You might need to add an additional tablespoon of almond milk for the last few pancakes, because the batter will thicken on standing, due to the psyllium husk.

Serve warm, with a dollop of coconut yogurt, and possibly some orange slices, a drizzle of maple syrup, and scattered with toasted nuts and seeds.

Optional stir-ins:
To switch up the pancakes each time, perhaps try adding a pinch of ground ginger and some orange zest, a tablespoon of ground flaxseeds, some maca powder, or anything else you might fancy! So long as the basic ratio isn't altered drastically it'll all work perfectly.

103

WATERCRESS, SPINACH + AVOCADO SOUP WITH SCALLIONS, LIME + PINE NUT SALSA

P G D SF V

This soup is delicious served hot, or chilled the following day. Thickening the soup with avocado rather than potato gives it a wonderfully creamy texture, and enriches it with good fats, ensuring the soup is satisfying and suitably filling. The zingy salsa isn't essential, but really takes the soup to a new level!

 MAKES 4 GENEROUS BOWLFULS

CHEWS WILL VARY DEPENDING ON TOPPINGS AND GARNISHES

INGREDIENTS
+ 2 tablespoons organic canola oil, or cooking oil of your choice
+ 1 onion, minced
+ 4 celery stalks, finely chopped
+ 1 quart hot vegetable stock
+ 4 packed cups baby spinach
+ 4 packed cups watercress
+ freshly grated nutmeg
+ 1 teaspoon English mustard powder

+ 1 ripe avocado, seeded and peeled
+ salt and pepper

SALSA (OPTIONAL)
+ 2 tablespoons pine nuts
+ 4 scallions, finely sliced
+ small handful of curly parsley, chopped
+ 2 tablespoons extra virgin olive oil
+ 1 lime

Heat the oil in a large saucepan. Add the onion and celery and gently sauté for 10 to 15 minutes, until soft and somewhat translucent. Season with salt and pepper.

Pour in the stock and bring to a boil. Add the spinach and watercress, some freshly grated nutmeg, and the mustard powder, and stir. Only let to boil for about 2 minutes (in order to preserve the vibrant green color, it's best to cook this soup quickly).

Turn off the heat and let the soup cool a little before blending with a hand blender.

Add the avocado and blend again. You want the smoothest, silkiest texture possible.

Enjoy immediately, or chill as quickly as you can (again, to preserve the color). If you're planning to enjoy the soup cold (it is unbelievably refreshing), chill overnight if possible. A few hours won't do; it needs to be seriously cold!

For the salsa, toast the pine nuts in a dry skillet for a few minutes, until just golden, then cool. Chop together the scallions, parsley, and pine nuts, or blitz in a food processor. Stir in the olive oil, lime juice, and some salt and pepper. Drizzle your soup with the salsa to bring everything to life! The salsa will keep in an airtight container in the fridge for 2 days.

CHLODNIK

This is a chilled beet soup from Poland. It is wonderfully refreshing and the vibrant color makes it a real show-stopper. A lot of the water content comes from the raw cucumber blitzed in at the end, rather than from stock, making it super healthy. We use kefir or coconut yogurt in place of crème fraîche, adding a gentle sourness to offset the natural sweetness of the beets, and a brilliant dose of probiotics for gut health. Use the firmest, freshest beets you can. With a variety of toppings to add, you can really make this soup your own.

SERVES 4

CHEWS WILL VARY DEPENDING ON TOPPINGS AND GARNISHES

INGREDIENTS

+ 2 tablespoons cold-pressed canola oil
+ 1 onion, diced
+ 3 beets, peeled and grated
+ 1 1/4 cups hot vegetable stock
+ 1 cucumber, peeled and chopped
+ 1 cup kefir or coconut yogurt
+ salt and pepper

OPTIONAL TOPPINGS

+ hard-boiled eggs, chopped
+ smoked mackerel, flaked (omit for vegetarians)
+ fresh dill
+ lemon
+ pickled cucumber (see overleaf)

Heat the oil in a large saucepan. Add the onion and gently sauté for approximately 10 minutes, or until translucent and soft.

Meanwhile, prepare the beets. The juice will go everywhere, so don't wear white and if you have any disposable gloves, put them on!

Add the beets to the softened onion, season with salt and pepper, and pour in the hot vegetable stock.

Simmer gently, covered, for approximately 15 minutes, until the beets are soft. Turn off the heat and let cool a little. At this point it won't look like there is enough liquid, but the water content of a whole cucumber, added in a moment, as well as the kefir, will be sufficient.

Transfer the cooled soup to a high-power blender. Add the cucumber and the kefir. Blend on high power until totally smooth (perhaps even straining through a fine sieve or some cheesecloth if it doesn't look perfectly smooth after blitzing).

Chill the soup for at least 6 hours, ideally overnight. It must be super cold before eating.

Top with your choice of chopped hard-boiled egg, flaked smoked mackerel, lots of chopped dill, freshly squeezed lemon juice, and some pickled cucumber.

continued overleaf ➞

QUICK PICKLED CUCUMBER

+ $1/3$ cup water
+ $1/4$ cup white wine vinegar
+ 1 tablespoon honey
+ 2 slices of lemon

+ $1/2$ cucumber
+ fresh dill, chopped
+ salt and pepper

Gently heat the water, vinegar, honey, and lemon slices in a small saucepan until the honey has dissolved. Season to taste.

Meanwhile, cut the cucumber in half lengthwise, remove the watery center using a melon baller, and finely slice into thin "half-moons." Place in a bowl with the dill.

Let the pickling liquor cool slightly so that it is warm rather than hot, then pour it over the cucumber and dill.

Chill until needed. The pickled cucumber will keep for up to a week in the fridge.

MACKEREL WITH FENNEL, ZUCCHINI + RADISH

This simple summer lunch is so delicious and fresh. The salad has a wonderful crunchy texture thanks to the raw fennel, zucchini, and radish, and a brilliant zing from the lemon.

SERVES 2

APPROXIMATELY 35 CHEWS PER MOUTHFUL

INGREDIENTS

+ 3 to 4 mackerel fillets, depending on size
+ 2 tablespoons extra virgin olive oil
+ $\frac{1}{2}$ unwaxed organic lemon, finely sliced
+ 2 scallions, finely sliced
+ 1 tablespoon capers

FOR THE SALAD

+ 1 bulb of fennel, halved and very thinly sliced (fronds reserved for garnishing)
+ 1 zucchini, halved lengthwise and finely sliced or ribboned using a vegetable peeler
+ 6 radishes, finely sliced
+ leaves from a few sprigs of fresh thyme
+ 2 tablespoons extra virgin olive oil
+ juice of $\frac{1}{2}$ lemon
+ salt and pepper

First, prepare the salad by mixing all the ingredients together in a bowl. Place the salad in the fridge while you cook the mackerel. This salad can happily be dressed up to 2 hours in advance, and is extra refreshing served chilled.

Check the mackerel fillet for small bones and remove any using tweezers. Season the skin side of each fillet.

Heat the oil in a nonstick skillet. When it is good and hot, add the mackerel fillets skin-side down—they should sizzle immediately. You might need to gently press them down with a spatula as they curl up in the heat.

Lightly season the exposed flesh side. Keep the heat high and cook for 3 to 4 minutes.

Flip the fillets over, turning the heat down slightly. Add the slices of lemon and scallions. Cook for 2 minutes, then turn off the heat and add the capers. Let the fish rest for a moment while you dress each plate with the salad.

Serve the mackerel on top of the salad, making sure to scrape all the delicious pan juices and oils onto it, as this is where a huge amount of flavor hides. The lemon slices are to be eaten too—these are totally delicious with the salty capers and piquant onions, contrasting and complementing the oily fish.

SMOKED MACKEREL WITH PINK SAUERKRAUT, WATERCRESS + CRUNCHY KEFIR DRESSING

P   G   D   SF

This is one of my all-time favorite lunches; it's the perfect quick fix, so satisfying and nourishing, yet wonderfully light thanks to the fresh, cool crunch of the sauerkraut and the crunchy kefir dressing. The batch of dressing here is a little more than you will need, but it will keep for three days in the fridge (just give it a stir) and is sensational dolloped on top of almost everything. The sauerkraut is a pleasure to make, and once you have a jar on the go it will last and last for weeks on end.

SERVES 1

APPROXIMATELY 35 CHEWS PER MOUTHFUL

INGREDIENTS

+ 1 generous handful of watercress
+ 1 tablespoon extra virgin olive oil
+ 1 teaspoon apple cider vinegar
+ 1 or 2 smoked mackerel fillets
+ 2 heaped tablespoons pink sauerkraut (see page 110)

+ 2 tablespoons of crunchy kefir dressing (see page 110)
+ 2 scallions, finely sliced
+ wedge of lemon for squeezing
+ salt and pepper

For this quick fix lunch, simply toss the watercress with the olive oil and apple cider vinegar. Season with salt and pepper and assemble on a plate with the smoked mackerel, sauerkraut, and crunchy kefir dressing. Scatter with the scallions and finish with a squeeze of lemon juice.

continued overleaf ⟶

CRUNCHY KEFIR DRESSING

This crunchy dressing is similar to a tzatziki or raita. The addition of kefir gives it a savory, tangy flavor, as well as an awesome serving of probiotics. If you would prefer not to use dairy, coconut yogurt loosened with a little nut m*lk (see page 92) works perfectly. Mint and dill marry very well with the coolness of the kefir and the cucumber. Simply combine all the ingredients in a bowl and serve.

INGREDIENTS

+ 1 celery stalk, finely diced
+ 4-inch chunk of cucumber, finely diced
+ 4 sprigs of mint, chopped
+ 6 sprigs of dill, chopped
+ 1/4 garlic clove
+ 1/2 cup kefir, or a combination of kefir and Greek yogurt or coconut yogurt
+ juice of 1/2 lemon

PINK SAUERKRAUT

Sauerkraut is fermented cabbage and I'm obsessed with it; try making it on a weekend afternoon when you have a little more time. Sauerkraut can be flavored with any number of herbs and spices, but for versatility's sake, I love plain sauerkraut, as it goes with almost everything. This recipe fills a 1-quart flip-top Kilner jar, with a little extra (depending on the size of the cabbages used); pack any surplus into a smaller, recycled jam jar with a lid.

INGREDIENTS

+ 2 white cabbages, finely shredded
+ 1 red cabbage, finely shredded
+ 2 tablespoons coarse or flaky sea salt

YOU WILL ALSO NEED

+ rubber gloves
+ 1-quart Kilner jar

Add the cabbage to a large mixing bowl with the salt. Don your gloves (crucial for red cabbage), and crush it all together using your hands for 6 to 10 minutes until the mixture is soaking wet. (It never ceases to amaze me how much water is released.)

Pack the cabbage, along with all the salty juices, into your jar as tightly as possible. To ensure the cabbage stays below the water line, I trim the cabbage base (washing it first) into a disk so that it fits neatly inside the neck of the jar, and place this on top. As you close the lid of the jar, it should compress against the cabbage disk, exerting extra pressure on the sauerkraut below and submerging it perfectly.

Keep the sauerkraut at room temperature for 3 to 4 days. During this time it will bubble and fizz slightly. "Burp" the jar each day (over the sink!). After 3 to 4 days, place in the fridge where it will keep for several months. You will notice how the flavor shifts over time.

COLLARD GREENS, LEEK + BUTTERNUT BROTH

 P G D SF V

This warming broth is hearty and comforting. If you are craving some extra sustenance, any cooked bean or legume makes a lovely addition (I favor haricot beans here), as does pearl barley. This recipe is incredibly versatile, as you can successfully adapt the vegetables to make use of what you have on hand. It's also great for batch cooking, to enjoy during the week.

➕ SERVES 2 HUNGRY PEOPLE

👄 APPROXIMATELY 40 CHEWS PER MOUTHFUL

INGREDIENTS

+ 2 tablespoons organic canola oil, or cooking oil of your choice
+ 1 onion, minced
+ 2 celery stalks, finely chopped
+ 1 garlic clove, crushed
+ few sprigs each of rosemary and thyme (ideally fresh, but dried is OK), leaves removed and chopped
+ 1 leek, sliced

+ ½ small butternut squash (or 1 sweet potato), peeled and diced into small cubes
+ 2 cups hot weak vegetable stock
+ 1 head of collard greens (or 2 cups kale, cavolo nero, or spinach), tough stalks removed, leaves rolled up and evenly sliced to create strips
+ 1 teaspoon Dijon mustard
+ salt and pepper

Warm the oil in a large saucepan over medium heat. Add the onion, celery, garlic, and herbs and sauté for 10 minutes or until soft.

Add the leeks to the pan (you can add another tablespoon of oil if necessary). It's ideal if you can let the leeks caramelize a little because this will add depth and complexity of flavor. You may want to increase the heat a little, but be sure to watch it carefully and stir every couple of minutes.

After a few minutes, add the squash. Continue to cook over medium heat for approximately 8 minutes.

Pour in the stock and cover with a lid. Let simmer gently for 10 to 15 minutes, until the sweet potato is cooked through.

Stir the shredded greens into the broth, and cook very gently for a further 3 to 5 minutes. If you are using kale, cook for a little longer. If you are using spinach, turn off the heat and just stir through until wilted.

Turn off the heat, stir in the mustard for a little kick, and tuck in.

SWEET POTATO SALAD WITH SPICY SEEDS, POMEGRANATE + CILANTRO

This salad is almost too beautiful to eat! The colors are amazing, and the complexity of textures quite extraordinary. The crunchy seeds and pomegranates against the softly roasted sweet potato are just awesome. It's all about the toppings here!

SERVES 4

APPROXIMATELY 40 CHEWS PER MOUTHFUL

INGREDIENTS

+ 4 sweet potatoes, sliced into disks about 1 $^1/_4$ inches thick
+ 1 tablespoon canola oil, or cooking oil of your choice
+ $^1/_4$ cup spicy seed mix (see page 114)
+ $^1/_4$ cup crunchy kefir dressing (see page 110)

+ 8 radishes, finely sliced
+ 6 scallions, finely sliced
+ $^1/_4$ cup pomegranate seeds
+ few sprigs of fresh cilantro, chopped
+ $^1/_2$ lemon, for squeezing
+ salt and pepper

Preheat the oven to 400°F and line a baking pan with nonstick parchment paper.

Spread the potato disks evenly on the baking pan. Drizzle with the oil and season with salt and pepper. Place in the oven and cook for approximately 25 to 30 minutes, or until caramelized around the edges and soft in the middle. Remove from the oven and let cool slightly before dressing the salad.

While the sweet potatoes are cooking and cooling make the seed mix and the dressing.

Layer all components on a large plate, reserving a little of everything for garnishing the top. Finish with a squeeze of lemon just before serving.

For an even easier midweek supper, simply bake whole sweet potatoes and enjoy with this assortment of toppings.

continued overleaf ➡

SPICY SEED MIX

This seed mixture is a fantastic way of injecting brilliant texture, color, and complexity of flavor into almost any salad. It will happily keep for a week sealed in an airtight food container, so doubling the recipe and keeping some handy is a great idea. You can simply use $1/2$ cup of whatever seeds you have on hand, but below I've listed my favorite combination.

INGREDIENTS

+ 2 tablespoons pumpkin seeds
+ 2 tablespoons sunflower seeds
+ 2 tablespoons unshelled hemp seeds
+ 2 tablespoons flaxseeds
+ 1 teaspoon coconut oil
+ 1 teaspoon dried red chile flakes
+ 1 teaspoon curry powder
+ 1 teaspoon ground turmeric
+ 1 teaspoon honey
+ pinch of sea salt

Preheat the oven to 375°F. Place the larger seeds on a baking pan and dry-roast for 3 to 4 minutes (I don't roast the flaxseeds as they are so little and tend to burn).

Heat the coconut oil in a large skillet over medium to high heat. Add all of the seeds, along with the spices, honey, and salt.

Keeping everything moving by shaking the pan constantly, cook for approximately 3 minutes, until the mixture has colored slightly and looks glossy from the oil, but dry.

Tip onto some nonstick parchment paper and spread out evenly to cool.

ROASTED CAULIFLOWER + ALMOND SOUP

 P G D SF V

This soup is so unbelievably creamy and thick it seems crazy to think it hasn't been blended with loads of heavy cream! It has a lovely velvety texture, and a deep complex flavor thanks to the roasted cauliflower.

+ MAKES 4 GENEROUS PORTIONS

CHEWS WILL VARY DEPENDING ON TOPPINGS AND GARNISHES

INGREDIENTS

For the roasted cauliflower:
+ 1 cauliflower, chopped into florets, stalk reserved, peeled and finely chopped
+ ¼ cup organic canola oil, divided
+ 1 onion, finely sliced
+ 1 celery stalk, finely sliced

+ 1 garlic clove, minced
+ few sprigs of fresh thyme, leaves stripped
+ 2 cups Plenish almond m*lk
+ 1 cup vegetable stock
+ handful of whole almonds
+ lemon juice
+ salt and pepper

Preheat the oven to 400°F.

Toss the cauliflower florets with 2 tablespoons of the oil on a baking pan. Season with salt and pepper and roast in the oven for 15 to 20 minutes, until colored. A little charring will add depth of flavor.

Meanwhile, make the soup. Heat the remaining oil in a medium/large saucepan, add the onion, celery, and garlic and gently sauté, keeping the heat low. Add the thyme leaves and the prepared cauliflower stalk. Season with salt and pepper.

Pour in the almond m*lk and vegetable stock. Heat gently up to smoking point, when you start to see some steam but just before it boils (a rapid boil can cause the milk to split).

Once the cauliflower is roasted, add it to the saucepan and continue to cook gently for 5 minutes. Turn off the oven.

Scatter the almonds onto a clean baking pan and dry-roast in the residual heat of the oven for 3 to 4 minutes, then coarsely chop.

Remove the soup from the heat. Let cool slightly before transferring to a jug blender and blending until totally smooth—the smoother, the better. Taste and adjust the seasoning accordingly.

Serve the soup in warmed bowls, garnished with a grinding of black pepper, some fresh thyme leaves, the chopped roasted almonds, and a generous squeeze of lemon juice to make everything sing.

ROASTED BROCCOLI WITH PRESERVED LEMON, ALMONDS + TAHINI LEMON DRESSING

G **SF** **V**

Roasting broccoli entirely transforms it. The slight charring adds a wonderful texture and flavor, which marries well with the salty and tart preserved lemon, and the creamy dressing. The dressing also makes a wonderful healthy dip.

 SERVES 2 TO 3 AS A MAIN COURSE, OR 4 IF PART OF A LARGER MEAL

APPROXIMATELY 25 CHEWS PER MOUTHFUL

INGREDIENTS

+ 1 head of broccoli, chopped into florets, stalk trimmed and sliced
+ 3 garlic cloves, finely sliced
+ 2 tablespoons olive oil
+ 2 tablespoons sliced almonds, or ¼ cup whole almonds
+ 1 preserved lemon, quartered, flesh separated from the skin and skin finely diced
+ 4 scallions, finely sliced
+ small bunch of curly parsley, chopped

FOR THE DRESSING

+ ¼ cup tahini
+ 2 tablespoons Greek yogurt, kefir, or coconut yogurt if you prefer dairy free
+ ¼ cup hot and light vegetable stock or bouillon
+ juice of 1 lemon
+ salt and pepper

Preheat the oven to 425°F, place a rack at the top of the oven, and line a baking pan with nonstick parchment paper.

In a bowl, toss the broccoli and garlic with the oil. Transfer to the lined pan, season with salt and pepper, and roast in the oven for approximately 10 minutes, until slightly charred yet retaining a firm texture.

While the broccoli is roasting, make the dressing by simply shaking up all the ingredients in a jam jar. This dressing is quite thick—one for dolloping rather than drizzling. If it looks a little too thick, simply add another tablespoon of vegetable stock.

Once the broccoli is roasted, remove from the oven. Slide the parchment paper, containing the broccoli, off the pan, and set aside to cool.

Scatter the almonds onto the baking pan and dry-roast for 3 to 4 minutes, then coarsely chop.

Finally, place the cooled broccoli on your chosen serving plate, dollop over the dressing, and scatter with the preserved lemon, scallions, parsley, and chopped almonds. A light drizzle of extra virgin olive oil makes a welcome final flourish, if you like!

LEEK + PEA FRITTATA WITH PEA SHOOTS, RADISH + SCALLIONS

(P) (G) (D) (**SF**) (V)

This protein-packed main has a natural sweetness from the peas and caramelized leeks. Nutritional yeast gives a cheesy flavor, yet remains dairy free. If, however, you adore cheese, a little scattering of grated sharp Cheddar, goat cheese, or Gruyère will be delicious. Will keep for two days in the fridge and is great as a portable lunch.

SERVES 2, OR 3 TO 4 PEOPLE IF PART OF A LARGER MEAL

APPROXIMATELY 35 CHEWS PER MOUTHFUL

INGREDIENTS

+ 2 tablespoons canola oil, or cooking oil of your choice, plus extra for drizzling
+ 1 leek, finely sliced
+ 1/2 cup frozen peas
+ 4 eggs
+ 1/4 cup Plenish almond m*lk

+ 6 sprigs of dill, chopped
+ 1 tablespoon nutritional yeast
+ 2 handfuls of pea shoots
+ juice of 1/2 lemon
+ 4 scallions, finely sliced (optional)
+ salt and pepper

Heat 1 tablespoon of oil in a medium nonstick skillet. Add the leek, cover, and sauté on medium heat for 10 to 15 minutes, until soft and slightly caramelized.

Meanwhile, fill and boil the kettle and place the peas in a sieve suspended over the sink. Once the kettle has boiled, carefully pour the boiling water over the peas to thaw and blanch. Let drain for a few minutes to dry, thus avoiding a soggy frittata.

Crack the eggs into a mixing bowl. Add the almond m*lk, dill, and yeast. Season with salt and pepper and whisk the mixture.

Let the leeks cool before stirring them into the egg mixture, along with the dry peas. Preheat the broiler.

Heat the remaining tablespoon of oil in the same skillet you used for the leeks. Tip in the egg, leek, and pea mixture. Keep the heat low and cook gently for 10 to 12 minutes.

When the frittata looks almost cooked through, but still has a slight wobble on top, place it under the preheated broiler for 2 minutes.

Transfer the frittata to a cutting board and let cool for 2 minutes before slicing.

Dress the pea shoots with a drizzle of oil, the lemon juice, and salt and pepper to taste. Either scatter these on top of the frittata or serve alongside it. Finely sliced scallions make a lovely additional topping if you have some on hand.

SPROUTED GREEN GOODNESS BOWL

Green on green on green. A wonderful variety of textures, tied together with a simple vinaigrette. The ingredients below are by no means definitive—this salad is absolutely a case of use-what's-on-hand. A tablespoon of sauerkraut (see page 110) goes well, too.

✚ SERVES 2

⊖ APPROXIMATELY 45 CHEWS PER MOUTHFUL

INGREDIENTS

+ ¹/₂ broccoli head, chopped into florets, stalk trimmed and sliced
+ 1 tablespoon pumpkin seeds
+ 1 tablespoon sunflower seeds
+ 1 small zucchini, sliced into ribbons
+ 1 ripe avocado, peeled, seeded and chopped
+ 2 scallions, finely sliced
+ 1 cup arugula, packed
+ handful of sprouting broccoli cress (or store-bought garden cress)
+ ¹/₂ cup sprouted green lentils or sprouted mung beans (see page 121)
+ small handful of soft herbs, such as chives and/or dill, chopped

For the vinaigrette dressing:
+ 3 tablespoons extra virgin olive oil
+ 1 tablespoon raw apple cider vinegar
+ 1 teaspoon Dijon mustard
+ 1 teaspoon liquid honey
+ salt and pepper

Optional:
+ 1 portion of poached or hot-smoked salmon, or 2 ¹/₄ oz goat cheese, crumbled
+ ¹/₂ lemon

First, combine all the dressing ingredients in an old jam jar, seal, and shake well to combine.

Bring a medium saucepan of salted water to a boil.

Once the water is boiling rapidly, add the broccoli and cook for no more than 2 to 3 minutes. Drain in a colander, and cool immediately under cold running water. Let the broccoli dry by spreading it out on a few sheets

of paper towel while you prepare the other ingredients.

In a dry skillet, toast the pumpkin and sunflower seeds until they brown slightly and start to "pop"; this should take only 2 to 3 minutes.

continued overleaf ⟶

In a large mixing bowl, combine with the arugula, garden cress, sprouted lentils or mung beans, and the chopped herbs. If you are flaking in some poached salmon or crumbling in some goat cheese, do so now. Add the cooked broccoli, some salt and pepper, and the dressing. You may or may not wish to use it all depending on personal preference.

Mix very well, then transfer to your serving bowl or pile onto plates. A squeeze of lemon juice over the top always brings out the best in a salad.

SPROUTING:

Sprouting beans and legumes not only brings out their wonderful nutty and earthy flavor better than cooking, in my opinion, but it retains a fabulous crunchy texture as well, which can enhance almost any salad. Sprouting makes the legume or bean easier to digest and enables us to assimilate more of its nutrient content too.

The length of time needed for soaking and sprouting can vary depending on the legume or bean in question, but for both green lentils and mung beans, simply soak in a generous amount of fresh water for 12 hours. After 12 hours, drain the lentils or beans, but do not rinse, and transfer either into a large Kilner jar, or a sprouting container. Cover the top with some cheesecloth, or a square of paper towel punctured with a few holes. Let stand in a quiet spot out of direct sunlight for approximately 48 to 72 hours, rolling the jar around once or twice during the sprouting period; the sprouting time will be shorter if the weather is warmer. If the jar starts to look dry, pour in a little fresh water, swirl it around, and drain it out just to moisten things. You will see signs of germination after 24 hours. Once sprouted, transfer to a clean, airtight food container, seal it, and keep in the fridge for up to a week. You can scatter the sprouts on everything!

122

MISO-ROASTED VEGETABLES + TEMPEH WITH BLACK SESAME + LIME

This salad is wonderfully hearty, but the dressing makes it light and zingy. Roasting the tempeh and vegetables in a miso glaze really enhances their flavor, and boosts the umami quality of the dish. Choose a dark miso which is refrigerated and unpasteurized, to ensure you are getting the probiotic benefits. Great for batch cooking, so scale up for portable lunches. The dressing will keep happily in an airtight container in the fridge for a week.

SERVES 3

APPROXIMATELY 48 CHEWS PER MOUTHFUL

INGREDIENTS
+ 4 organic carrots, peeled and chopped
+ 1/2 cauliflower, chopped into florets
+ 6 round shallots, quartered with the end intact so they hold together
+ optional: 6 whole garlic cloves, unpeeled
+ 7oz fresh organic tempeh, crumbled into chunks of various sizes
+ small bunch of fresh cilantro, chopped
+ black sesame seeds
+ juice of 1 lime

For the miso roasting glaze:
+ 1 tablespoon mild canola oil, or cooking oil of your choice

+ 1 teaspoon miso paste
+ 1 teaspoon liquid honey
+ salt and pepper

For the lime and miso dressing:
+ small chunk of fresh ginger root, peeled and grated
+ 1 teaspoon miso paste
+ 1 teaspoon liquid honey
+ 1 tablespoon toasted sesame oil
+ 1 tablespoon mild canola oil
+ 1 tablespoon rice vinegar or white wine vinegar

continued overleaf ➡

Preheat the oven to 400°F, with an oven rack near the top, and line a baking pan with nonstick parchment paper.

Combine the vegetables, garlic cloves, and tempeh in a large mixing bowl.

Mix the roasting glaze ingredients together in a separate bowl. Pour the glaze evenly over vegetables and tempeh, and mix well, massaging the glaze into the vegetables to coat evenly.

Tip the glazed vegetables and tempeh onto the prepared baking pan and cook at the top of the oven for 20 minutes, until richly caramelized. If you prefer a little more caramelization or charring, turn the broiler on during for the last few minutes. Once cooked, remove from the oven and let cool slightly.

Meanwhile, make the dressing. Combine all the ingredients in a jar, seal, and shake well.

Pile the roasted vegetables and tempeh onto a serving platter. Scatter with the chopped cilantro and sesame seeds and douse generously with the dressing. Squeeze over plenty of lime juice, or serve with lime wedges on the side.

SPICY MARINATED KALE WITH QUINOA + WALNUTS

This salad is wholesome and delicious, and packs a spicy punch. You can easily prepare it in advance; unlike other salads that would wilt unappetizingly, this salad softens and marinates, making it even more delicious. Perfect if you have friends over, or if you want to prepare tomorrow's lunch in advance.

SERVES 3 TO 4

APPROXIMATELY 40 CHEWS PER MOUTHFUL

INGREDIENTS

+ ³/₄ cup quinoa
+ 2 packed cups kale, chopped and tough central stalks removed
+ ¹/₄ cup walnuts
+ ¹/₄ cup crumbled feta (optional)
+ fresh herbs, chopped (optional)

For the dressing:
+ 3 tablespoons extra virgin olive oil
+ 1 small shallot, finely diced
+ ¹/₂ red chile (or more if you love the heat!)
+ pinch of cayenne pepper and paprika
+ 1 teaspoon liquid honey
+ 1 lemon, zest and juice
+ salt and pepper

Preheat the oven to 375°F (for toasting the walnuts later).

Place the quinoa in a suitably sized saucepan (it quadruples in volume as it cooks). Cover with plenty of salted water or light vegetable stock and bring to a boil. (A teaspoon of bouillon powder in the water is perfect here, lifting the salad's overall flavor.) Simmer the quinoa for 20 to 25 minutes, or until it has swollen and "sprouted."

Meanwhile, place the kale in a colander over the sink.

Once the quinoa is cooked, simply pour it into the colander over the kale, which will encourage the kale to wilt nicely. Allow the quinoa and kale to billow off steam for a few moments, then spread it out on sheets of paper towel to dry off further.

To make the dressing, combine all the ingredients in a jam jar, seal, and shake well. Toast the walnuts in the oven for approximately 5 minutes; this will enhance their flavor, and give them a crunchier texture.

Put the quinoa and kale into a large salad bowl and add the dressing. Using your hands, massage the dressing into the salad for 2 minutes. This encourages the kale to soften and the quinoa to absorb the flavors. Season to taste.

Coarsely chop the toasted walnuts and add to the bowl, reserving a few for garnishing. Crumble in the feta now, if using, as well as any chopped soft herbs you may have.

Serve garnished with the extra walnuts. Alternatively the salad will keep happily in the fridge for 2 to 3 days.

GINGER, TAMARI + HONEY SALMON WITH PURPLE SPROUTING BROCCOLI + EGG-FRIED RICE

This supper is wholesome and bursting with flavor. It's a perfect combination of good fat, protein, smart carbs, and dark green vegetables. If you have some rice already cooked it will only take 15 minutes; if you need to cook some first, you can throw the broccoli into the same pot four minutes from the end of cooking to save doing dishes!

SERVES 2

APPROXIMATELY 40 CHEWS PER MOUTHFUL

INGREDIENTS
+ small chunk of fresh ginger root, peeled and grated
+ 1 tablespoon honey
+ 1 tablespoon tamari
+ 1 tablespoon sesame oil
+ juice of 1/2 lime
+ 1 teaspoon nam pla (optional)
+ 2 skin-on salmon portions
+ 1 teaspoon sesame seeds (optional)

For the egg-fried rice:
+ 1 tablespoon sesame or coconut oil
+ 1 shallot, minced
+ 1 red chile, finely diced
+ 1/2 cup cooked wholegrain rice
+ 1 cup baby spinach (optional)
+ small bunch of fresh cilantro, chopped
+ 1 large egg
+ salt and pepper
+ 10 spears of purple sprouting broccoli

Prepare the salmon. Make a marinade by whisking the grated ginger with the wet ingredients. Pat the salmon dry and submerge in the marinade, coating well. Let marinate for 30 minutes.

Prepare the egg-fried rice next. Heat the oil in a small saucepan, and gently sauté the shallot and chile for 5 minutes. Add the cooked rice, spinach, if using, chopped cilantro, and seasoning. Crack in the egg and stir-fry for 1 minute. Keep the rice warm.

Heat a nonstick skillet. When hot, add the salmon portions skin-side down—they should sizzle immediately. Do not add all the marinade yet, as the honey will burn. Lightly

season the flesh side of the fish. Turn down the heat to medium and continue to cook for 5 minutes. Placing a saucepan lid over the pan will stop too much splattering and help steam-cook the salmon.

Meanwhile, bring a pot of salted water to a boil and cook the broccoli for 2 minutes, to retain some bite.

After 5 minutes, flip the salmon over and add the rest of the marinade, along with the sesame seeds, if using. Cook for 1 minute, then turn off the heat and let the salmon rest while you plate up the rice and broccoli, followed by the salmon portions, the delicious pan juices (crucial!), and a squeeze of lime.

BROCCOLI POWER BALLS

This is my new favorite recipe! I don't have much of a sweet tooth, and for a snack I tend to prefer something savory rather than something sweet. There are plenty of recipes out there for sweet "energy balls." Well, here's an awesome recipe for a savory one. Packed with plant-based proteins and plenty of green vegetable goodness.

MAKES 16 BALLS

APPROXIMATELY 28 CHEWS PER MOUTHFUL

INGREDIENTS

+ ½ cup pumpkin seeds
+ 2 cups packed raw baby spinach
+ 1 head of broccoli, chopped into florets, stalk trimmed and sliced
+ 1 heaped teaspoon English mustard
+ freshly grated nutmeg

+ 2 heaped tablespoons nutritional yeast
+ 2 eggs
+ ½ cup ground almonds
+ 1 teaspoon psyllium husk (optional)
+ salt and pepper

Preheat the oven to 350°F and line a cookie sheet with nonstick parchment paper.

Scatter the pumpkin seeds onto a baking pan and toast in the oven for 6 minutes, until beginning to "pop." Once toasted, tip the seeds into a food processor.

Start blitzing the seeds. With the motor running, add a small handful of spinach followed by a few florets of broccoli, then spinach, then broccoli, etc. Turn off the motor and push the mixture down if necessary, and season with salt and pepper.

With the motor running again, add the mustard, nutmeg, nutritional yeast, and eggs.

Finally, add the ground almonds. The almonds add flavor as well as protein, but, crucially, help absorb excess moisture.

Let the mixture stand for 20 minutes, after which it will have firmed up slightly and you should be able to roll it in your hands. It is a damp mixture, but shouldn't feel sloppy.

If for some reason it feels too wet to handle, add more ground almonds, until the desired consistency is achieved. Alternatively, add a teaspoon of psyllium husk, mix well, and wait 10 minutes for the mixture to thicken before rolling into balls.

Place the balls on the cookie sheet and bake in the oven for 12 minutes. Once cooked, transfer to a cooling rack.

These will keep happily in the fridge for 4 days sealed in an airtight container. They can also be frozen.

RAW VEGAN NUTTY OAT SQUARES

 P G D ● V

These squares are crunchy, salty, and slightly sweet all at the same time. They are packed with good energy and are brilliant for a breakfast on the go, or a delicious snack. The orange flavor is divine with the toasted nuts. Keeps in the fridge for a week.

+ MAKES APPROXIMATELY 30, DEPENDING ON SIZE

◯ APPROXIMATELY 30 CHEWS PER MOUTHFUL

INGREDIENTS

+ 1 $^1/_3$ cup mixed nuts—we used hazelnuts and walnuts
+ $^1/_3$ cup mixed seeds—we used chia, sunflower, and pumpkin
+ $^1/_2$ cup jumbo oats (gluten free if you wish)
+ pinch of ground cinnamon
+ pinch of salt
+ $^1/_3$ cup coconut oil
+ 2 heaped tablespoons goji berries
+ 4 to 5 medjool dates (depending on size and sweetness preference), pitted and coarsely chopped
+ vanilla extract
+ zest of 1 orange

Preheat the oven to 350°F.

Toast the nuts on a baking pan for 3 minutes. This is absolutely crucial for the overall flavor. It also helps dry out the nuts and gives each bite a crunchier texture. Add the seeds and continue toasting for 2 more minutes.

Let the nuts and seeds cool slightly, then tip them into a food processor and add the oats, cinnamon, and salt.

Warm the coconut oil in a small saucepan, then add the goji berries and dates and let them soften. Add the vanilla extract and the orange zest. It's key that the dried fruit softens in the warming oil. This will enable it to be blitzed to a finer paste, which will therefore bind the ingredients much better—the dates, goji berries, and coconut oil are the "glue" to these raw nutty squares.

Add this warm mixture to the food processor and blend well. Now wait 5 minutes and then blitz again. It will blitz more finely once cooler.

Line a suitable food container or small baking pan with nonstick parchment paper (I used an airtight food container, 8 x 5 inches in size, with a lid). Add the mixture and flatten well. The key here is to really press and flatten the top. If it's not pressed enough it won't stick together. You can use the palm of your hand here to add some pressure! Cover and let chill in the fridge for at least 4 hours, but ideally overnight.

Slice and enjoy. These will keep happily in a sealed food container in the fridge for a week. They are best enjoyed straight from the fridge.

Play around with new combinations of nuts, seeds, and dried fruit. Perhaps try adding some almond extract in place of the orange zest. Or, some dried apple in place of the goji berries to go well with the cinnamon. Ground ginger is always delicious, too. Get creative!

6. THE PROGRAMS

5:2 JUICE PLAN

The 5:2 diet is a weight management plan centered around intermittent fasting. You reduce your calorie intake two days per week and resume normal, healthy eating the remaining five days.

For this 5:2 juice plan you will replace food with juice on your two reduced-calorie days. This will restrict your daily calorie intake to approximately 500 calories for women and 600 calories for men.

We have many clients who use our juice-based solution for the 5:2, as it fits into their busy lifestyle with minimal effort. You can download a success tracker from: www.plenishcleanse.com/TrackMySuccess

We recommend spreading your juices out to 1 glass (approximately 8 fl oz/1 cup or half of one recipe) about every other hour to keep blood sugar levels balanced. This breaks down as shown in the chart below.

DAY 1	♂ **WOMEN**		8 fl oz Fit p. 66	8 fl oz Fresh p. 72
	♀ **MEN**	8 fl oz Fit p. 66	8 fl oz Sing p. 70	8 fl oz Balance p. 73
DAY 2	♂ **WOMEN**		8 fl oz Deep p. 66	8 fl oz Focus p. 72
	♀ **MEN**	8 fl oz Deep p. 66	8 fl oz Balance p. 73	8 fl oz Smart p. 69

MORNING

WOMEN

You will need a total of 1 quart of juice per day (choose any of the fruitless or green juices to keep calories under 500) and 16 fl oz (2 cups) of nut m*lk per day, such as plain cashew or almond. 1 quart of juice is equivalent to two juice recipes, and 16 fl oz of nut m*lk is equivalent to one nut m*lk recipe, all of which can be found in Chapter 3.

MEN

You will need a total of 1 ½ quarts of juice per day (choose any of the fruitless or green juices to keep calories under 500) and 16 fl oz (2 cups) of nut m*lk per day, such as plain cashew or almond. 1 ½ quarts of juice is equivalent to three juice recipes, and 16 fl oz of nut m*lk is equivalent to one nut m*lk recipe, all of which can be found in Chapter 3.

8 fl oz Deep p. 66		8 fl oz Focus p. 72	16 fl oz Almond m*lk p. 92
8 fl oz Deep p. 66	8 fl oz Strength p. 73	8 fl oz Smart p. 69	16 fl oz Almond m*lk p. 92
8 fl oz Fit p. 66		8 fl oz Fresh p. 72	16 fl oz Almond m*lk p. 92
8 fl oz Fit p. 66	8 fl oz Sing p. 70	8 fl oz Strength p. 73	16 fl oz Almond m*lk p. 92

NIGHT

GUT HEALTH WEEK

For the full run-down on how a healthy gut affects performance, see pages 32–37. This sample menu incorporates a lot of the foods recommended for supporting a healthy gut. It's full of whole foods, vegetables, fermented foods, and easy-to-assimilate juices. This plan is simply a suggestion for a Monday–Friday work week. Feel free to switch it around, based on the gut-healthy foods that suit your tastes.

	MONDAY	TUESDAY
BREAKFAST	Juice of your choice	Nut M*lk of your choice
LUNCH	Sprouted Green Goodness Bowl p. 119	Juice of your choice
SNACK	Juice of your choice or Raw Vegan Nutty Oat Squares p. 128	Juice of your choice or Raw Vegan Nutty Oat Squares p. 128
DINNER	Chlodnik p. 104	Watercress, Spinach + Avocado Soup with Scallions, Lime + Pine Nut Salsa p. 103

You can add in nuts, seeds, and fresh vegetables and fruit. We also reccomend a daily good-quality probiotic like Plenish Water+.

 If you regularly suffer from digestive issues, I'd highly recommend seeing a nutritional therapist to help diagnose any food intolerances that can trigger immune reactions and unpleasant digestive symptoms.

WEDNESDAY	THURSDAY	FRIDAY
Juice of your choice	Juice of your choice	Banana + Blueberry Pancakes with Coconut Yogurt + Maple Syrup p. 102
Miso-Roasted Vegetables + Tempeh with Black Sesame + Lime p. 122	Juice of your choice	Sprouted Green Goodness Bowl p. 119
Juice of your choice or Raw Vegan Nutty Oat Squares p. 128	Juice of your choice or Raw Vegan Nutty Oat Squares p. 128	Juice of your choice or Raw Vegan Nutty Oat Squares p. 128
Sweet Potato Salad with Spicy Seeds, Pomegranate + Cilantro p. 112	Roasted Cauliflower + Almond Soup p. 115	Collard Greens, Leek + Butternut Broth p. 111

EAT YOURSELF SMART WEEK

If you need a bit of extra focus or brainpower, see pages 25-31. You'll learn how feeding your brain with the right nutrition can have a positive effect on mental performance and health–like consuming enough "thinking greens" or using healthy oils for healthy minds. This plan is just a suggestion for a Monday-Friday work week. Feel free to switch it around, based on the brain-healthy foods to suit your tastes.

	MONDAY	TUESDAY
BREAKFAST	Spiced Carrot + Walnut Breakfast Loaf p. 98	Juice of your choice
LUNCH	Collard Greens, Leek + Butternut Broth p. 111	Watercress, Spinach + Avocado Soup with Scallions, Lime + Pine Nut Salsa p. 103
SNACK	Fit p. 66	Smart p. 69
DINNER	Roasted Broccoli, with Preserved Lemon, Almonds + Tahini Lemon Dressing p. 116	Mackerel with Fennel, Zucchini + Radish p. 107

A few extra tips:
- Eat at regular intervals
- Stay hydrated and watch alcohol intake (which dehydrates you and can make you feel tired)
- Load up on vegetables
- Eat complex, not simple carbs (think whole grains, oats, legumes, not the refined sugars found in processed cookies, or the refined flour used in white pasta, etc.)
- Make your ZZZs a priority and get enough sleep.

WEDNESDAY	THURSDAY	FRIDAY
The Sarah (smoothie) p. 53	Baked Eggs with Mushrooms, Spinach, Goat Cheese + Chile p. 100	Walnut Coffee M*lk p. 88
Spicy Marinated Kale with Quinoa + Walnuts p. 125	Juice of your choice	Sprouted Green Goodness Bowl p. 119
Focus p. 72	Broccoli Power Balls p. 127	Strength p. 73
Leek + Pea Frittata with Pea Shoots, Radish + Scallions p. 118	Chlodnik p. 104	Ginger, Tamari + Honey Salmon with Purple Sprouting Broccoli + Egg-fried Rice p. 126

INDEX

BIBLIOGRAPHY

CHAPTER 2: GUT + BRAIN SCIENCE

· Ashraf, R., Shah, N. P. (2014), Immune system stimulation by probiotic microorganisms, Crit. Rev. Food Sci. Nutr.

· Fetissov, S. O., Dechelotte, P. (2011), The new link between gut-brain axis and neuropsychiatric disorders, Curr. Opin. Clin. Nutr. Metab. Care.

· Heras-Sandoval, D. et al. (2016), Role of docosahexaenoic acid in the modulation of glial cells in Alzheimer's disease, J. Neuroinflammation.

· Lyte, M. (2013), Microbial endocrinology in the microbiome-gut-brain axis: how bacterial production and utilization of neurochemicals influence behavior, PLoS. Pathog. 9.

· Ramakrishna, B. S. (2013), Role of the gut microbiota in human nutrition and metabolism, J. Gastroenterol. Hepatol.

· Sapolsky, R. M., *Why Zebras Don't Get Ulcers*, 3rd edition (2004), First Holt Paperbacks.

· Yarandi et al. (2016), Modulatory effects of gut microbiota on the central nervous system: how the gut could play a role in neuropsychiatric health and diseases, J. Neurogastroenterol. Motil.

ABOUT PLENISH

When you're focused on what's ahead, it's important to make sure that your body can keep up with you. You need energy to fuel your drive, keep you healthy, and push you forward. Our raw, delicious juices, dairy-free nut m*lks, and probiotic waters are packed with nutrients and designed to Plenish, so that just like our juices, you can thrive under pressure.

Plenish is now the number one contemporary wellness brand in the UK. You can visit **www.plenishcleanse.com** to check out our whole range of cleanse programs, cold-pressed juices, nut m*lks, and other healthy drinks. Additionally, our products are stocked at the following retailers:

Amazon www.amazon.co.uk

Boots www.boots.com

Booths www.booths.co.uk

Harvey Nichols www.harveynichols.com

Ocado. www.ocado.com

Planet Organic www.planetorganic.com

Selfridges www.selfridges.com

Waitrose www.waitrose.com

Wholefoods www.wholefoodsmarket.com

ABOUT KARA

A former Condé Nast exec, Kara Rosen moved from New York to London in 2009. After overhauling her health by following a mostly plant-based, veg-centric diet, Kara struggled to find high-integrity, cold-pressed juices, and plant-based products in London.

Never one to stand still, Kara started Plenish in 2012 with an online shop selling a range of cold-pressed juices, juice cleanses, and 5:2 diet programs designed by nutritional therapists. After huge success, the retail world caught on, and started selling Plenish juices in a grab-and-go format.

The brand and Kara have been featured in top publications such as *Vogue*, *Grazia*, *GQ*, *ES Magazine*, and *Metro*. Plenish has been named "Britain's Coolest Brand" two years in a row (2015 and 2016) by Cool brands, won the 'Great Taste Awards' (2015) and "Best New Brand" from the World Beverage Innovation Awards (2015). Their juice cleanses have also won the Soil Association's BOOM awards for best cleanse in the UK.

Kara's first book **Plenish: juices to boost, cleanse, and heal** was published by Mitchell Beazley in 2015.

ACKNOWLEDGMENTS

To my husband, Leon Diamond, as a fellow entrepreneur and business owner, your perseverance continues to inspire me. Thanks for letting Plenish dominate our pillow talk for the last five years, helping me celebrate the wins and bounce back from the losses. Thank you also for being an incredible balance partner.

To my munchkin, Belle, for your beaming pride every time we see a Plenish product on a shelf, your fearless nature, and your curiosity to try everything. There is no one I want to work harder for than you.

To the Plenish team for your belief in the dream, your sweat, and laughs. You are such bright stars and I'm constantly inspired by how you "bring it" every day.

To Hannah Templeman for your fine-tuned taste buds and creativity!

To Dr. Wendy Goldberg and Patti Rosen for your brilliant editing.

To Peter Dubens and Andrew Wolfson for your continued support and believing that Plenish is the future of healthy drinks.

To Chris Britton for your highly solicited advice.

To Eve Kalinik for sharing your expertise and integrity with us. You are the triple threat!

To Andy Medd, Dan Broadwood, and Christian Cervantes for the only brains and advice I rate higher than my own mother's.

COOKING NOTES

Measures are given in cups throughout. This relates to a standard 8-ounce measuring cup.

Use free-range eggs throughout, unless otherwise specified.

This book includes juices and dishes made with nuts and nut derivatives. It is advisable for customers with known allergic reactions to nuts and nut derivatives and those who may be potentially vulnerable to these allergies, such as pregnant and nursing mothers, invalids, the elderly, babies, and children, to avoid dishes made with nuts and nut oils. It is also prudent to check the labels of ready-made ingredients for the possible inclusion of nut derivatives.